W9-AKD-714

The Fragile Thread

ALISKE WEBB

STARBURST PUBLISHERS
Lancaster, Pennsylvania

To schedule Author appearances write: Author Appearances,
Starburst Promotions, P.O. Box 4123 Lancaster, Pennsylvania 17604
or call (717) 293-0939

Website: www.starburstpublishers.com

CREDITS:
Cover design by David Marty Design
Text design and composition by John Reinhardt Book Design

We, the Publisher and Author, declare that to the best of our
knowledge all material (quoted or not) contained herein is accurate,
and we shall not be held liable for the same.

THE FRAGILE THREAD
Copyright ©1998 by Aliske Webb
All rights reserved

This book may not be used or reproduced in any manner, in whole or
in part, stored in a retrieval system or transmitted in any form by any
means, electronic, mechanical, photocopy, recording, or otherwise,
without written permission of the publisher, except as provided by
USA copyright law.

First Printing, October 1998
ISBN: 0-914984-543
Library of Congress Catalog Number
Printed in the United States of America

TO

Eleanor Roosevelt
for raising the consciousness of women
with stength and dignity

Oprah Winfrey
for raising the compassion of women
with humor and courage

Audrey Hepburn
for raising the conscience of women
with elegance and grace

Heroines all who have shared
their journeys with us

The fragile thread
of dignity and grace that unites
the human tapestry . . .

Harper Lee

ONE

Grandmother's Garden

MY NAME IS AGGIE AND I LIVE IN CLAREVILLE. I was forty-seven when I moved here. The only man I had ever loved was dead. My beloved mother-in-law, mentor and guide, Grama, had passed away only two years before. My two daughters were grown, one working and one away at college. My son was grown too, and living on the west coast.

And I'm the fool who put all her savings into opening a quilt shop on Main Street just before they were about to tear it down. It was going to be my dream, my retirement project. I was going to be the creative center for women in the community. I was going to be true north, the spiritual guide, a lighthouse.

But when did things ever turn out the way we expect?

Clareville was going to be the perfect spot for me. It had been my husband's home town, and it was the place where Grama had lived. I signed the real estate contract quickly and could barely contain my excitement at the prospect of moving and starting a new line of work in a peaceful little town, far away from the pressures of big city living. No more tall buildings gorging thousands of people in every morning at eight and spitting them out again at five. After I'd spent years urging other people to move forward in life, to go out and engage the world, I was finally following my own best advice.

On closing day in Clareville, I retrieved the keys from the real estate agent, drove around for half an hour before I found a parking space close to the shop and finally approached the portal to

1

my latest destiny. There was an old-fashioned lock and chain on the front door. I reached out and touched the chain. Rusty red powder stained my pale fingertips. I stood staring at the crimson dust on the metal and was suddenly mesmerized by the weighty links. It was like a sign, like a memory in a dream, long forgotten, half-submerged. Transfixed, I thought, "What am I doing here?" I stared through the wavy reflection of my face in the glass of the door, and remembered.

A few months earlier, I had read a story in a medical journal about a class of children who were so autistic that they couldn't even stand up by themselves. If you stood them up, they simply fell over, not even shielding their eyes or making any effort to brace their fall. One day the teachers strung a thick rope across the room and found that if they stood the kids up so that they were holding the rope, eventually they could walk across the room. Somehow those brave little incapacitated souls found the strength to cross their unfathomable distance. They had nothing going for them except the courage to trust their footsteps to the reassuring rope. It was a small and thankful miracle. Over the months the teachers gradually strung up thinner and thinner pieces of rope, until they were using almost invisible fishing line. And the children would walk across the room, if only they could hold onto the "rope". Finally, in an act of unprecedented trust and ingenuity, the teachers cut the thread-like line into twelve inch pieces and each child continued to walk, still clutching their lifeline.

It was a testament of faith. That we can make the journey to the other side if we just hold onto that fragile thread of hope that binds us together with the rest of humanity.

Shortly after that I told my partners I was leaving the clinic. I explained that I realized it was time to heal myself, to reconnect with the world around me. I, too, had to trust my own tentative steps to move forward in the flow of life again. I needed to find wisdom and truth, not just answers. I thought the fresh air and green trees in Clareville would provide me with a positive and creative environment. After all, it had been a long cold winter and it was spring again. I thought I had every good reason to make changes. My colleagues were disappointed but understood and wished me well. In the end, it took several months to wind down my counselling practise and find new therapists for all my clients. It was an ironic compliment to me that no one was happy about my leaving, except me. It reminded me of the Bob Newhart show years ago in which he played a psychologist. His patients didn't think he was very helpful, but they didn't want to leave.

I laughed at the thought and my reflection in the glass door jarred me back to awareness. I wiped my rust-stained fingers on my jeans. Excited, optimistic and only a little intimidated, I placed the key in the rusty latch and after too much fiddling, the hasp finally snapped open and I separated the chain. What a cumbersome device this is, I thought. Why didn't they just put a deadbolt on the door? This will have to be replaced, I decided, making the first of many mental notes. Then I stepped across the threshold into the cool dark interior. It was as motionless as a funeral home, where only whispering spirits reside in the obsequious shadows.

I held my breath and realized, "I am alone. Again."

It had been ten years, almost to the day, since Jack died. I missed him still, the love of my life, my soulmate. When he passed away I thought the world would end. I always assumed we would be married forever. I thought our days were strung together like notes on a keyboard. One would follow the other in a natural progression, each growing clearer and higher. I believed we were tied together with a strong and almost invisible thread, as strong as piano wire. No matter how hard you twist and strain against the thin strand, it will not break. Your hands may grow bloody as the bonds cut deeper into your flesh, and soul. But the wire will not break. I didn't know it would have to be severed by death.

The air inside the shop hung still and damp. It was like stepping into an Egyptian tomb, and a chill ran up my spine. There were lifeless artifacts all around me, caught in the morning light like beetles encased in amber. Even the dust motes had settled in the motionless air.

I took my first deep breath and, letting it out, began to set the place, and myself, in motion again.

CLAREVILLE IS A SMALL COLONIAL TOWN, built around an old square. The focus of the square is a pretty little park with huge oak and maple trees. It's a pleasant green space full of twittering birds and manic squirrels. The original town planners defined the area of the common by erecting four stone and ornamental wrought iron gates in the middle of each side, north, south, east and west. Since there has never been a fence around the park anyway, the gates have stood open and rusted for generations. A bronze plaque on the north gate bears the date 1752 and the name Dalton J. Rimple, first mayor of Clareville. A crisscross of footpaths which were originally dirt, and then cement slab, wander through the park from each gate. When the cement fell into disrepair, the paths were covered over with tar and now the asphalt is ragged and lumpy with weeds thrusting through the cracks. In the southeast corner of the park there is a wooden gazebo, a turn-of-the-century bandstand fallen into disrepair and disuse. The park is edged on three sides by narrow streets and on the fourth, the south side, by a red brick gothic church and the granite town hall driveway and steps. With its stained glass windows and tall steeple dominating the landscape, it appears that, originally at least, the church was mightier than the state. After the town had built the church and then the town hall, I learned, it was up to Mayor Rimple to push through setting aside the five acre park. The issue had been hotly debated. A visionary before his time, Rimple stood and filibustered Council for fourteen straight hours before everyone finally gave up, gave him his park and went home.

Outside the park, the central streets are lined with brownstone two- and three-storey Federal style buildings. The street opposite the town hall has earlier, rough-hewn grey granite slab buildings on each corner with a row of ugly postwar buildings between. It's an eclectic mixture of architectural styles of houses shops, restaurants and service businesses, most of which have been there for many, many years. It's the antique heart of a still-growing community.

Beyond the town square are several blocks of mixed commercial and residence-lined streets which comprise the original downtown area. And beyond that, the newer town stretches out into suburbs, with a less developed sense of planning. In most American colonial towns the streets were laid out in easy grids like the precise seam-lines in a "Log Cabin" quilt. We inherited many of those original orderly neighborhoods where many of our grandparents could look down a street and be comforted by seeing a small tree-lined stretch of neighborhood houses. Our own parents could easily find us; they knew we were playing three blocks over and one block down, at Tony's.

It's curious that nowadays new streets are constructed as curves and cul de sacs, with no view of the neighbors. I suspect it's a misguided notion of privacy and that bothers me. You can't see your neighbors' private troubles. But you can't see their emergencies, either. I believe the safety of our streets is directly related to the number of eyes watching the street. Crimes are more easily committed in isolated areas where no one is watching. Most people do want to see their neighbors, I think we're a nosy species. We just don't want the neighbors to *see us*. It's called privacy. Or isolation may be more like it. Do we really want to observe the world passing by but not be involved in it or touch it, for fear it may touch back?

In the old neighborhood we didn't always like our neighbors. But you knew who they were and if there was an emergency, you knew who was home and who you could run to for help. That's a neighborhood. Even if you didn't like someone, you would help them anyway. That's a community.

And come to think of it, that's a society. A great society.

My limited savings and a small inheritance from Grama allowed me to buy a small fabric shop on the town square, in the middle of the block right on Main Street. The shop is directly opposite the western gate of the park so it faces east, into the morning sun. I was really lucky. The property had just come on the market. There was one other buyer who was eager to close the deal which was why I had to move fast. The couple who owned the prime shopfront said they didn't really like the other buyer but they wanted to retire soon and move to Georgia. They were sad to leave Clareville. It had been home for forty years. They said they felt like they were deserting their customers, so they were relieved that I was going to keep it as a fabric shop. Maybe they thought the other guy was going to put up a donut franchise!

So I took over the old fabric shop.

I renamed it Grama's Quilt Shop, placed an order for a new wooden sign and blithely moved into the cute two-bedroom apartment upstairs. It was smaller than the family house the children and I lived in for so long. Packing at that house was a good opportunity to jettison my excess baggage, emotional and otherwise. At times it was wrenching to decide what to take, what to throw away. But out with the old, in with the new, I said to myself as I carried out bags of stuff, some to recycling, some to Goodwill, some to friends. I realized that I'd spent twenty-five years acquiring stuff which never gave me the permanence and security that I thought it would. In the end I kept only what I couldn't replace—things like family photos, Grama's quilts, my computer disks, Jack's state championship game-winning football from college, my mother's crystal. Rather than feeling bereft, I was amazed at how en-lightened I felt. I felt as young and new as a college-kid leaving the weight of home for the first time. It was the first time in years I felt so free and unencumbered.

I bought new smaller furniture for the apartment. It had a lovely bay window with sheer cafe curtains and it overlooked what I soon regarded as my own personal haven in the budding greenery of the park across the street. I quickly acquired the habit of sitting on that front windowseat with my coffee every morning for a few restful minutes before the busy day began. It was just what I was looking for. There was something so peaceful about watching the birds flit around the reassuring arms of the old oak trees that even on the most frantic days I would wake up fifteen minutes earlier than I needed to, just so I wouldn't miss my morning commune with nature.

It was soon Spring Break for my youngest daughter, Susan, and she came home from teacher's college. My elder daughter, Jennifer, took a week's vacation from the bank and both girls helped me paint and clean. I know I shouldn't call them "girls" anymore. They are women. But they will always be my girls. Just as, no matter how ancient and wonderfully wise I may hope to become, I will probably always be just "Mom" to them.

The fabric shop, I learned, began life a century ago as a drugstore. It had several incarnations since. The goods on sale changed but the store itself basically stayed the same. The alcoves along both side walls were lined with eight foot high deep wooden shelves. These had originally held cupboards and drawers filled with arcane and long-forgotten remedies. The previous owners left the original shelving but it was stained a dark walnut color and lent a cold gloominess to the store even in broad daylight. So, we started the renovation by moving everything upstairs that wasn't nailed down. We painted the ten foot high ornamental tin ceiling a clean bright white and then painted the shelves to match and after the paint dried we filled them with bolts of cloth. The top shelf is too high to reach so Sue suggested putting plants and country knickknacks up there.

There was also a long counter running along one side where the cash register is now. We left it in its original dark wood finish. The new white paint made the shop a hundred percent brighter so I thought we could leave some of the antique wood finish without its making the store dark inside. There was a large, poorly-lit cutting table in the center, over which we hung two cheerful Tiffany lamps for extra light during evening hours or overcast days. The wide plank floors were uneven and worn but there wasn't much I could do about that. Besides, the creaking floor would always tell me when someone entered the shop.

In the end, Grama's Quilt Shop took on a nice comfy country store look. As it turned out, it was almost too cozy and peaceful.

During the weeks before Jennifer and Susan arrived I had talked with all the manufacturers' sales reps and enjoyed picking out wonderful new bolts of fabric to stock my new enterprise. I was like a kid in a candy store surrounded by delicious, tempting treats. I wanted one of everything! Of course the buying was fun but then there was the problem of what to do with the fabric the previous owners had left behind. Bolts of chintz and wool and knits that quilters don't often use. Most quilts are made from one hundred percent cotton fabric. It's tradition. It's a more "forgiving" and flexible fabric to work with. And besides, cotton is a natural fiber. It keeps us grounded to the earth, to living growing things.

In the end, Jennifer suggested a yard sale or "yard-age sale" of the unusable stuff at ten cents a yard just to be rid of it.

"But that's part of my inventory I bought with the place!" I protested.

"Mom, some of this stuff came over with the Mayflower," Jennifer objected.

"If only it had," Susan interrupted. "Then it might be worth something just for having survived this long!"

"It's not even that it's ugly," Jennifer continued. "It simply won't sell to quilters. You have to remember what business you are in—the quilting business—not warehousing! And every square foot of merchandise space has to produce a profitable margin. Sell this stuff off and replace it with what quilters want. Remember the Platinum Rule—do unto others as *they want* to be done unto! Grama was a great quilter and she would have wanted . . ."

"I know! Cotton." I nodded reluctantly.

She was right of course, my ever-practical financial wizard daughter. I should know better than to argue with a business degree graduate. Then again, perhaps an opening week special sale would bring in some early customers, I decided, so we spent an evening making large colorful posters for the front window.

In the meantime, Hobbes, our six-year old stripey-gray cat, had a grand old time exploring his new surroundings. In spite of the fact that his tubby stomach wobbles when he walks, Hobbes found a lot of intriguing gadgets to snatch and chase around the shop, cosy places to knead into suitable sleeping spots and interesting activities to poke his uninvited nose into. All in all, he approved of the colored cloth business and settled happily into the role of Shop Cat. With that infallible instinct cats have for striking a picturesque pose, he installed himself in the front window as if to do his bit in attracting customers. This cat has presence. Besides, what could be more appealing than the sight of a big dozy cat asleep on a quilt!

As a final touch when the renovation was complete, we hung Grama's last quilt, *Hearts and Roses*, on the wall behind the cash desk. It's my best treasure, the one she made for me. It's not a masterpiece quilt, it's too full of whimsy, personality and idiosyncracies, but there are dozens of memories in the fabrics she chose for her last quilt. There are scraps from all of our lives and from hers. I recognize pieces from many of the clothes we wore, and I love to look at it and recall the times and places associated with them. Plain clothes, fancy dress clothes. Clothes with happy memories and clothes with painful ones. But there are also many older scraps that were from her own generation about which I can only speculate. Of course, we didn't know it would be her last quilt. We might have paid more attention. Like the faces of distant relations in photo albums that we forget to identify before their names are lost, I never thought to ask Grama for her own recollections that were imbedded in the quilt.

Perhaps that is the attraction of old quilts. Their patterns connect us, in a visceral sort of way to themselves. Quilts made from old clothing scraps are made from part of us. They are us. They are like the scars on our bodies that are memories of wounds and the scars on our hearts that are memories of pain. They are like the photos we keep in albums and the bundles of letters tied with ribbon that capture the joy of relationships. They are like ticket-stubs and playbills and yellow newspaper clippings that catalogue the events of our lives. The quilters are distant and remembered, yet connected to us still, even though they are gone.

Like Grama.

Grama had been a prodigious quilter. When she died, I lost touch with her guiding spirit and realized how much I missed the peaceful times we spent quilting together over the years. I hoped I could recapture the spirit of quilting and communing with other women by opening my own shop. Grama's quilts are a family treasure. Every one is rich and full of life. Somehow I guess you can't stitch a quilt and not move forward into life. Grama was a member of that long line of grandmother souls who stitched their love and creative beauty into their quilts. It was their ritual meditation on life, their way of making every moment holy and complete. Imagine the power contained in a scrap quilt made for a child. The cloth came from the worn and washed clothes of all her relations, cut before she was born, sewn with a prayer in every stitch and wrapped around the infant. It's the way of grandmothers.

I still talk to Grama. Often enough to feel reassured but not often enough to be put away in a padded room. I think she is still around, watching over us. Maybe believing *that* will get me put away.

When my husband Jack died, along with every other heartwrenching emotion I felt, I hated the thought that all the wonderful love he had for his family would die with him. Not that we would stop loving him, but because he was dead, his love would die too. In the same way, I'm not so much afraid of dying, but I hate to think that the love I have for my children will die when I end. I want to live forever so I can go on emanating love to them. It was Grama who said, "Jack will never leave. His love will always be wrapped around you and the children, keeping you safe and warm." And there have been times since then that I have felt an unmistakable, overpowering and *directed* love surround me, and I knew it was Jack. Or the hand of God clothed in Jack's embrace.

Grama will never leave us either.

Especially after the wake we gave her! If I had any sense I would be embarrassed about it but I'm not. The family gathered at The Morrison Funeral Chapel. We're not a huge group but we're noisy. After the restrained hugs and whispers we all sat down to chat quietly. There were many relatives and friends we hadn't seen in a long while. So there was news to catch up on. Eventually current events turned to recollections and stories about Grama. Aunt Phyllis recalled the first time Grama, as a new bride, decided to bake a raisin pie as a surprise for Grandad. She didn't know a lot about cooking but she went ahead anyway. She poured the raisins into her piecrust and baked it. What she didn't know was that she should have added some sugar to make a syrup. The pie cooked and the raisins turned out as hard as buckshot but Grandad dutifully chewed his way through the whole thing so as not to hurt her feelings. It was family anecdote that you could break your teeth on one of Grama's pies. We all tittered. That led Uncle Gord to tell a joke Grama would have loved and we laughed out loud. Well, that was it, we were off. After that we told jokes and stories and laughed until tears ran down our faces. Tears of relief, and joy.

Uncle Bernie who never made it past grade school but now runs his own wood-working company in Vermont recited poems by heart from Grama's favorite poets: Robert Frost, Robert Burns and Robert Service. "The Sublime, the Scot, and the Silly," she used to call them. She liked poets named Bob! We sang old songs and sorely wished we had an upright piano to pound on. We needed one to keep us in key. It sounded as though we were having a party and indeed we were celebrating Grama's life. There is a rightness when an old soul dies and is buried by her adult children and relations. It's in the proper course of time and nature. She has fulfilled her destiny and raised up a new generation to maturity.

The funeral chapel staff finally came and discreetly closed our parlor doors and we carried on regardless. There would be enough sad days of missing her later. In her honor it was a time of joy and happy memory. It's what she would have wanted. Her spirit was with us that day and maybe she still hangs around just to hear our jokes, to make sure the family laughter didn't die with her.

The night of the funeral, I remember feeling that she was tucking me gently into bed. It was the first of many visits. I felt her warm soft hand caress my temple as she whispered, "Thank you, Aggie dear." Despite my sad and heavy heart, I drifted off to peaceful sleep. Sleep well, Grama.

That was three years ago now and I sigh with resignation whenever I think of her. But then again, as Somerset Maugham once wrote: "I can find no more comfortable frame of mind for the conduct of life than a humorous resignation." Grama would have agreed.

ON THE SATURDAY EVENING before Opening Day of the shop on Monday, when all the exhausting work was finished, I stood for a few quiet moments looking out the shop door. A warm spring twilight had crept up on us. The trees in the park across the street were stark black silhouettes against a dark blue sky. The girls joined me. I turned and we stood together relaxing and admiring our labor.

"Looks good, Mom," said Jennifer, congratulating me.

"Fantastic!" exclaimed Susan. "You have the best looking shop on Main Street."

"Thanks to the two of you," I said, acknowledging my gratitude for their willing help

"Nah. It was nothing," Jennifer assured me.

"Now all I need are some customers," I said with worry, chewing a knuckle.

"You'll do great," Jennifer asserted, patting my shoulder. She's the eternally optimistic one in the family. Well, perhaps she's not so much an optimist as she is a firey and determined brunette.

"I don't know," I fretted. Finally faced with the imminent opening of the shop, suddenly I was struck with stage fright. "I'm beginning to think this might have been a colossal mistake. I must have been crazy to have uprooted myself like this. I thought I was past my mid-life crazies! I don't know anything about running a quilt shop. Now that the exciting honeymoon of renovating the place is over, reality has set in. It's as if I've married a stranger! I just don't know if I'm doing the right thing."

"We never do," said a voice from behind me. We all turned around in surprise to find a tiny, white-haired woman in a Hunter Green tracksuit standing just outside the open shop door. A small purple towel was draped over her shoulder. "Just remember that everything you are seeking, is seeking you," she said with a friendly smile. "Hello," she continued as she ran her hand through her touseled hair which stood out in every direction, in an attempt to calm it down. "My name is Jo, short for Josephelia. Although the only one who ever called me that was my mother. So you'd better just call me Jo. Welcome to Clareville. You have a beautiful shop here. When do you open? We've been watching you renovate." She put her hand out to shake as she stepped inside.

"Why, thank you. Who's 'we?' " I stammered in surprise, taking her hand automatically but forgetting to introduce myself.

"Oh, you know, everyone." She laughed, seeing my startled expression. " Don't worry. You're not in the Twilight Zone. It's just the usual small town busybodies. I'm surprised the welcome wagon hasn't been here yet. Everyone's dying of curiosity to know why on earth you would move here now."

"Why? Is it an election year?" Jennifer joked.

Jo laughed and waved her hand. "Oh. Everybody just chalks it up to you being city folk. You know. Don't let them bother you or wear you down! Anyway, it's nice to see a fresh face on the old square. If you're open now, I need some thread." She pointed to the rack behind us.

"Of course. Yes. That's great. Regular or quilting," I blurted, finally remembering my manners. "My name is Aggie. It's nice to meet you. These are my daughters, Jennifer and Susan." I gestured to each of them. They nodded a quick "Hi."

Jo returned the nod. "Quilting," she replied to my earlier question. "Red, if you have it."

Jennifer handed it to her. "Is this okay?"

"Perfect. There you go. Three new dollar bills for your first sale. You can frame them if you like. That seems to be traditional for shop keepers, isn't it? Sometimes I wish I'd kept the first dollar I ever earned. Maybe these will bring you luck. People say 'luck is for rabbits'. But if someone hung my paws from a keyring I wouldn't feel very lucky. Luck is simply when preparation meets opportunity. You'll make your own luck. Looks like you're well prepared. See you!" She waved goodbye and disappeared out the door again.

There was a cool emptiness in the shop after she had gone, as if a fresh breeze had suddenly blown in and then just as suddenly blown out again. Jennifer and I looked at each other, then burst out laughing.

"Whew!" Jen breathed.

"She forgot her change," remarked Susan, looking down at the coins in her hand. She bounced the coins on her palm, unsure what to do with them. I just shrugged. In the end she dropped them into a Cancer Society donation box which sat next to the cash register.

"I have a feeling she'll be back," Jennifer observed. "Yeah, for sure," she predicted with a laugh. She stuck a pin in the three dollar bills and tacked them to the wall. "For luck," she said. "And I'll cross my fingers for you anyway, Mom!"

"Interesting thought. Everything you are seeking is seeking you," Susan repeated quietly.

THE WEEK HAD GONE BY too quickly and we were all exhausted. That evening was our last night together before the girls would return home on Sunday. Funny that. "Going home" used to mean coming to me, now it means going from me. They are grown up and have lives of their own to lead. Jennifer was happily employed at a bank in the city and had moved into her own apartment. She was fairly serious about her current boyfriend, Jim. My son Robbie was in his final year studying oceanography in college out West and Susan was away at teacher's college. I've managed to get them this far, hopefully I've done my job. Adolescence was a lot like a circus high-wire act for all of us. It was full of excitement, full of danger and required years of practising the same moves, the same skills over and over. At the time, I was their practise net which allowed them to try and fall until they achieved their footing. All I can do now is be a safety net if they ever need me. They are talented, strong young people who have capable and confident steps. Yet there's a wistful sadness to the end of that time in a parent's life. There are days when you want to do it all over again, day by fractious day, and pay more attention to each moment of sunshine and shadow as it passes. There's a release to it also, like a sigh of relief after a storm. So I refused to be a sad empty-nester. They will always be in my heart and thoughts but I had to worry about myself for a while, I realized. There must be lots more left for me to do out there in the world now that the intensive mothering days are over.

"Well, here we are girls," I said, placing a teapot and mugs on the cutting table in the center of the shop. While the tea steeped I voiced my conflicting thoughts.

"You know, if you had told me a year ago that I would be sitting here now, in a new apartment, in a new town, with a new business to run, I would have said you were crazy. New, new, new! Sometimes I long for something old and familiar. I feel like I just want to curl up in one of Grama's cozy quilts and have everything go away. Sometimes I just can't believe I did this." Even in the short time they had been back, I had grown used to Jennifer and Susan being with me again and their departure was going to leave me facing this adventure alone. Although we had visited with Grama for years in the seniors' residence, I'd never lived in Clareville and I was still a stranger in a strange land. This was Jack's hometown. I had no emotional ties to my own.

"Mom, you *wanted* life to be different," Susan reminded me.

"This is the new goal you set for yourself. Everything will be fine."

"This is going to be good for you," Jennifer reassured me. "You needed to get out of your comfort zone, remember. With Susan and me gone, it's good for you to have something else to worry about. It'll keep the long distance telephone bills down!"

I cupped my hands around my mug waiting to fill it. The mug was a gift at the going-away party my friends and colleagues in the city threw for me before I left. They knew I was casting everything to the wind and opening a quilt shop in Clareville. There were mixed reactions to my decision. Some said, "What on earth are you doing!" and tactfully didn't add, "You must be crazy." Some said, "You're so brave," and then confessed, "I wish I could—" I knew that some of them would stay in touch but I also knew that many would drop away when time and distance made it inconvenient to visit, or when the strangeness of my new life made it too unfamiliar and awkward to keep the bonds of commonality strong. It was something I had to accept about my decision. I was a chrysalis leaving the secure shell, a snake leaving its outgrown skin, and nothing would ever be the same again.

"Are you planning to give some quilting lessons in the shop?" Jennifer asked, changing the topic.

"I'm not a teacher," I objected. "I'm not that good a quilter to teach."

"Mom, you know a lot about quilting. Besides, you know that when you teach something, you also learn it yourself. So why not have a go. You don't have to be as good as Grama was to teach beginners," Susan admonished me.

"You're right," I sighed. I am always proud of my girls' maturity but at that moment, hearing their wisdom somehow made me feel childish and stubborn. It's hard to hear your own advice coming back at you. It's hard to feel incompetent again at mid life. At my age, it was hard to admit I *needed* to hear the advice.

Looking around my—dare-I-say-the-word "new"— shop it struck me that our roles had reversed. The girls were now supporting and reassuring me in my hour -of doubt. And it was an easy and natural transition—they just walked into the role, now that they are women. I envied the apparent ease of their transition. But it's different for me, I thought, attempting to rationalize the difficulty of my position. They have other older women, even me, to use as role models. With Grama gone, I have no model to follow into my own role as matriarch of the family, apprentice crone of the community.

Grama's death had been a watershed in many ways. She was the glue that held the family together and I have a long way to go to fill her shoes. I'm now the oldest female relation of the family and the mantle is one I don't yet know how to bear with the dignity, wisdom and humor that she did. To my knowledge there aren't any courses in "Matriarchy 101." It's a role I suppose I'm going to have to grow into, inch-by-inch and day-by-day. Somewhere perhaps there is a path that will lead me back to my grandmother's.

The tea was ready but I was still distracted as I began to pour it into our mugs and the first mug nearly overflowed. I laughed, as it reminded me of the old Zen story about a learned professor who visited a temple in Japan. He sought knowledge and guidance from the resident master. The zen master willingly obliged and invited the professor to have tea with him but as soon as he had seated himself, the professor began talking on-and-on about what he knew about zen philosophy. The master said nothing as he poured tea into his guest's teacup. The professor hardly even noticed and kept on talking. Suddenly he realized that the master was still pouring tea—even though the cup was overflowing and spilling out over the floor. Yet the master kept on pouring. "Stop! Look what you are doing!" cried the professor. The zen master looked up calmly and said, "Just as the cup cannot hold any more tea when it is full, how can I teach you anything when your mind is already filled?"

I realized I had been pouring out more than just the tea.

The girls were right. It was true that I had wanted this change.

Although it seemed sudden, it had taken me almost a year to make the move. As I looked at the rainbow of colors around me, I saw that the shop was bright and shining. It was a promise-filled beginning. Like the rain-washed earth, it offered a fresh start just as I was reaching for one, I thought in surprise and I was filled with pride at all the work we had done. All of a sudden I felt a weight lift from my shoulders and I could breathe. I took a deep breath. And another.

Jennifer and Susan were walking around the shop, talking to each other, leaving me to my ruminations. I heard their soft conversation as they picked out fabrics they liked and imagined another quilt project they could make, if they had the time. I looked at Grama's quilt hanging on the wall and wondered what she would say right now.

Then it was as though I saw her, moving naturally and easily through our day-to-day spaces like an affectionate lingering shade. She was sitting in great-grandmother Lake's rocking chair which I'd placed near the front window. I put it there as a display rack for quilts. She was wearing the worn beige cardigan ("Beige goes with everything, dear") that she always wore, pockets stuffed with tissues, pencil stubs and other bric-a-brac. I love her dearly but she had no fashion sense, or if she did she left it behind somewhere in her youth. I heard her say with her familiar gentle and amused smile as she rocked back and forth, "Keep moving, dear. You know water can't freeze if it's moving. Keep moving forward." She was right of course.

I took another deep breath and felt an expansiveness open up inside myself. It was like unlocking and opening a cupboard.

Open. That was the word, I thought. That was the clue to moving forward in life. To receive tea, I reminded myself, you have to hold an empty cup. You have to be open to the future and to possiblity. Being open allows you to soften yourself to gratitude and your own vulnerability. You have to be willing to surrender to temporary uncertainty, to not knowing exactly where you are going. After all, if the certainties of life are temporary, so too are the uncertainties. Something can eventually be known from them. And the only way to do this is to have faith. Faith that ultimately there will be a positive outcome. As William James said: "Believe that life is worth living and your belief will help create the fact." To do what you want to do in life, you have to "let go," to feel the force of your unconscious, and engage the world head on.

"I think I'll start a quilt," I said impulsively, thinking of Grama.

"Great idea, Mom!" Jennifer encouraged me with a hug. They had rejoined me at the cutting table.

"Terrific," Susan echoed.

"Yeah. I'll make a 'sampler' quilt," I announced.

In a "sampler" style quilt, as the name implies, each block is a different pattern or a sample of several traditional quilt block designs. It's a good quilt for beginners because each pattern teaches a basic quilting technique such as piecing, applique, making clean points, sewing curves and so on. It's a gradual initiation, a gentle step-by-step process. By the time the quilter finishes, she has mastered every quilting technique she will ever need to make any kind of quilt she desires. Along with a paintbox of colored fabric, she then has a toolbox which allows her to build her creative dreams. A person may lie under a quilt and dream, but only the quilter gets to dream into her quilt.

"Yes. I'll do a sampler. You know, for practise," I repeated.

"Mom, nothing is 'for practice,'" Jennifer quoted Grama to me. "Everything in life is the real thing."

"Oh, oh. The chickens are coming home to roost!" I laughed as I heard another of Grama's favorite expressions being quoted to me. I was surprised to realize how often Grama must come into Jennifer and Susan's thoughts. Perhaps it was because we were in her space, so to speak, a quilting space. After all, the shop was named for her. Grama had taught them how to quilt and she also taught them about life. I'm glad they paid attention to her lessons.

I reflected and then said with inspiration, "Okay, then I'll call it my 'example' quilt. Ex-ample. 'Ex' as in 'out of,' and 'ample' as in abundance. So this will be my quilt-out-of-abundance! Is that okay?"

"That's better. That sounds like a way to see everything in a more positive light. I like it!" Jennifer exclaimed.

"Me too," nodded Susan.

"And the first block I'll make will be a *Grandmother's Garden*," I declared.

"In honor of Grama. That's a great idea." Susan caught my inspiration immediately.

"A beautiful place to start," Jennifer agreed.

We spent the rest of the evening talking about fabric and colors, and about men of course. There was no one special in Susan's life at that time. She was too busy at school, she said, but I think she was still just a little too shy in meeting people. She has time. Jennifer on the other hand, had her hands full with her job and with working out the normal adjustments of a relationship with her boyfriend Jim.

Eventually the girls went to bed but before I turned in I decided to cut out the pieces for my first quilt block. I sat on a wooden barstool at the big wide cutting table with just a single hanging lamp illuminating my work. The colored glass cast a rosy glowing circle around me. Everything was still and midnight quiet. Every little sound was magnified—the rolling of a pencil across the fabric, the crunching of scissors through cotton. It was like the silence of a Zen garden broken by the sound of water dropping onto a hollow bamboo pole. It focused my mind's wandering attention. There I was, like a small carefully-placed rock in the center of the garden, safely surrounded by bolts of fabric, all those potential quilts. It was a wonderfully warm and protected feeling. I sensed Grama's soothing presence as I worked, slowly and methodically. I understood why she often quilted late at night when the chores were done, when the world was smooth and tranquil. Her quilt hung in the shadows just beyond the circle of light as if she herself were standing back there in the wings waiting to step forward and speak if necessary.

It was a peaceful time, a time of innocence, a time of slumber before a storm.

GRANDMOTHER'S GARDEN WAS AN APPROPRIATE BLOCK with which to start my quilt. A garden is where we plant seeds and wait hopefully for a bountiful harvest. Everything that happens in a garden also happens in the human soul. There is sunshine that promotes growth, and frost that starts decay. Some seeds are nourished and thrive; others wither and die. Sometimes we have to cut back and prune in order to encourage healthy growth. There are unforeseen hailstorms, and yet overall there is an unrelenting thrust and lust for life and health despite the adversities which befall the garden, or the spirit. The garden will survive. You have to trust and have faith. A poet once said that the miracle of life waiting in the heart of a seed cannot be proved at once. Only time can prove the miracle that lies waiting. And the waiting needs faith.

I hadn't yet decided what the other blocks would be but I had the chance to "seed" my new quilt with scraps of old fabric and memories. The best part of the tiny estate Grama left to me was her fabric stash, her collection of fabric and scraps to use for quilting. Grama had very little in the way of the usual material possessions, but she did leave me *material*. Upstairs, under my bed, I had two large boxes and a bag of her fabric remnants she had gathered over the years and still hadn't used up. Like a collection of oil paintings or cherished books passed into new hands, Grama's colorful textiles continued to reveal her taste and personality, in what appealed to her, what she thought worthy of keeping. I figure if I quilt for the rest of my life, and if Jennifer and Susan continue to quilt, if we're careful we'll be able to "spice" every quilt we make with some of Grama's scrap treasures and still have some leftovers for the next generation! It's funny that she had some fabrics from the Twenties and Thirties which seemed nostalgic and antique to us. I looked at all the fabrics I bought and tried to imagine Jennifer and Susan, or their daughters and granddaughters, being nostalgic about the scraps which I may leave behind.

In the rings of hexagon-shaped pieces that make up the *Grandmother's Garden* block, I am the centermost green one. I am the seed in the center that is green and growing. "When you're green you are growing. When you're ripe, you rot!" Grama used to say with a laugh.

The first ring of six hexagons that surround my central green one are for my children. Two hexagons for each of them. Two blues for Robbie: a bright noble royal blue and a deep seagreen blue for his love of the ocean. Two yellows for Susan: a pale "peaches and cream" yellow and an optimistic lemon yellow, to remind her to add zest to her life. And two reds for Jennifer: a deep rose red and a passionate fire engine red, as a warning to the men in her tempestuous life! Blue, yellow, red. Bright primary colors because they are my shiny bright flowers, blossoms of love.

A second ring of twelve hexagons surrounds the first ring of my family. They represent the twelve hours on the clock face and the twelve months of the year to come—the time that measures our journey through life, our cycle of being. Each one a question mark of unknowns. Where was I last year, where will I be next? These hexagons are mottled gray, like fog or clouds that I can't see into, like the unseen future. And gray like a flagstone path through the garden, Grama's Garden. A family is also like a garden. In our family, Grama planted seeds without knowing how they would ever bloom. That's the faith we place in every new generation. The faith we have that time will render a fruitful balance in life.

The final eighteen hexagons in the outer ring are white on white, pale prints and delicate calicoes. These are for the spirit of all my friends and family who have passed away or who are far away but near to me in memory, whose wisdom and love still support me, still touch me. Grama, my husband Jack, Mom, Dad, my many friends. The background for all these hexagons, and people, is a lush forest green to symbolize the wide meadow of growth that surrounds us all.

Grandmother's Garden also reminds me that underneath every carefully tilled and fertilized plot of earth with its weeded and controlled arrangements of plants and flowers which we call an earthly garden, is God's garden. God's garden isn't at all like what we so-called gardeners produce. It is random, whimsical, disarrayed and yet perfectly natural. Everything grows as it is meant to. Just because there are weeds in it and the hedges are not neatly trimmed, or the plants are not laid out separately each according to its kind, doesn't mean it isn't a garden. A wild meadow looks chaotic but it is as much a garden as a sculptured, terraced park. I sometimes forget that when I am looking for perfection in the garden, the so-called "Garden of Eden" state of existence, that in fact God's garden is nothing like what we call a garden. In God's garden there is no order, there is only a process. And the process is called life.

There is "being" in the seed but the "doing" is in the growing. And doing requires engaging the environment and growing in the soil where you find yourself.

Grama once said, "Plant your garden with seeds of choice, or it will grow with seeds of chance that the wind blows in."

My life is my garden, my garden is my choice. I know that I cannot reap unless I sow. I don't know what the harvest will look like, but I'm open to its beauty and possibility, and I'm planting my garden with new choices.

TWO

Crossroads

JENNIFER WAS RIGHT OF COURSE. I did see Jo again. It should have occurred to me that, since she bought quilting thread, she must be a quilter. And where there's one, there must be more. Set a thief to catch a thief; set a quilter. . . . When she came into the store again, perhaps during my opening week "yard-age sale," I thought I would be ready for her. So I was delighted to see her early on opening day. It was bright and clear and the morning sun poured generously through the open front door.

"Hello Jo," I greeted her happily. "I'm glad to see you again. Sorry you caught us by surprise the other night. You must have thought we were all dodos!"

"That's okay. I must have scared the heck out of you, too. I looked frightful that night. I was hurrying from my exercise class to a meeting and saw your lights on and ran in," she replied affably. She was dressed in stylish denim slacks and a casual blouse studded with embroidered decals, beads and sequins. She was lightly made up and her hair was softly curled. Delicate silver bangles jangled musically on her arm. A different sight than the other evening to be sure. For a woman who appeared to be in her seventies, she was well put together.

"I'd like to chat with you if you have a few minutes," I suggested.

"Of course," she replied with a smile.

"As you know, I'm relatively new in town. And new in this business for that matter. You're the first quilter I've met in town and I want to be responsive to my customers, so I wanted to ask you—if you were me, what would you do with this business?"

24

It was a question Jack often asked. If you were me, what would you do? "Ask your way to success," he would say. "There is a lot of useful information out there in other people's experience. Ask your way to success," he would tell the younger executives. It's a question and an approach I found women responded to easily—unafraid and unembarrassed to ask for help, unselfish in giving help.

Jo looked at me closely, knitted her brows and put her hand to her chin. "Hmmm," she said. I waited. Jack also taught me to ask questions and then shut up and wait for the answer and not fill the silence with my impatience. He used to laugh at me because I would ask one question and then before he had a chance to answer, I'd light into another. "You don't talk fast enough!" was my defense. Sometimes I wonder how he put up with my steamroller eagerness.

My brief reverie about Jack was interrupted when Jo finally spoke.

"Well, I hadn't thought about another part time job, but I suppose I could do one evening class and a Saturday morning class. But not this Saturday. I have to go to a Board meeting. We can start next Tuesday evening. Seven o'clock until ten. Yes, Tuesdays are good. Okay, we'll see you then," she said and off she went out the door again.

"Wait!" I called to her it was too late to chase after her. A customer had walked up with three bolts of fabric to have some yardage cut. I was dumbstruck, again, by this diminuitive enigma but I had to turn away from the matter for the time being.

Some time later when I had a moment to think, I was alarmed when it suddenly occurred to me: I didn't know who Jo was or where she lived or even how to get in touch with her. And I seemed to have agreed to hire her as a quilting teacher. How had this happened?! All I wanted was advice and some contacts in town. Now what? And how was I going to find students for her class? For that matter, what was she going to teach? And how much would I have to pay her?

There I was, asking questions, but she had disappeared.

"Darn!" I said aloud to the empty shop. Or words to that effect. I looked at Grama's quilt and shook my head in disbelief.

"Now what!"

Well, first things first, I thought. I had several other customers off and on that day, so it was a while before I had an opportunity to close the store with a "Back in Five Minutes" sign and head for the local newspaper office down the street. I'll run an ad, was my brilliant and inspired thought. As Grama would say, "When life hands you scraps, make a quilt." That was the best way to turn a bizarre negative into a manageable positive.

"Good thing you came in today," the clerk said with an expressionless face as he handed me a form and a stub of pencil. He was a young man with a buzz cut except for one long lock of hair which hung over his pallid face. His T-shirt said "Surf Dude" and I thought, not likely. "Deadline's today for Friday's paper," he continued.

I filled in the form and handed my ad copy back to him.

"Do you happen to know a woman by the name of Jo, Josephelia perhaps. She's about five foot two—" I started to describe her on the off chance that he might recognize the description. I knew it was a stupid assumption that everyone in a small town knows everyone else.

"Yes. Sure. Jo," he replied, checking my form, counting words, without lifting his head. He moved his lips as he read.

"Would you know where she lives, or how I could contact her?" I asked hopefully.

"Nope. Can't think why I'd want to call her. She's always around town though. Not hard to find. Try the cable TV office. They know where everybody lives. That'll be $31.96 with tax, unless you want it to run again next week. You get a discount. Two weeks for $43.70."

"Okay. Two weeks." I opened my wallet.

"Cool," was all he said with either sarcasm or apathy, I'm not sure which.

As I RETURNED TO THE SHOP I saw a man standing outside, leaning casually against the door jam. He looked as if he was waiting for someone. Then I noticed he was wearing an official-looking grey shirt and trousers, crisply ironed like a police uniform. Oh, oh, I thought, wondering if something was wrong.

"Hello?" I said as I approached him. It was more of a question than a greeting.

"Howdy, M'am," he replied with a grin, reaching his hand up to his forehead and tipping what could have been an imaginary cowboy hat. "You're new in town," was his non-sequiter. He seemed to be amused by a private joke. I found myself infused with his inner merriment and smiled without even knowing why.

"Yes, officer, er," I stumbled, looking at the insignia on his shirt, "Fairbanks." He wasn't a police officer, but a fireman. "Oh," I said stupidly, "you're a fireman. I thought you were the Sheriff." He just smiled again. By then I had reached the sidewalk right beside him and he had to step out of the way so I could open the door. Since he made no motion to go away, but instead turned to follow me inside, over my shoulder I said, "Can I help you?" as I grappled with the key and chain, and opened the door.

"Been looking forward to your opening, M'am. Thought I'd take a look around if you don't mind," he replied.

"Help yourself," I offered with a smile and gestured into the shop. As he passed by I smelled a brief warm scent of cologne and even fainter perspiration. It was like the smell of fresh cut grass, reminding me of something I'd forgotten, but I couldn't quite remember what.

I hate to feel as though I'm being watched in a store and I didn't want to make him feel uncomfortable so I tidied and fiddled with bolts of fabric which were already pristinely lined up and straightened racks which were already four-square straight but I did watch him curiously out of the corner of my eye. Not often you find a man in a quilt shop, I thought to myself a little uneasily. Well, I guess it's not that unusual these days, but he didn't look like an artist or a . . . a . . . what else, I wondered.

"So what else would he look like?" I heard Grama ask. I saw her perched on the cutting table with her short legs dangling loosely over the side, swinging back and forth. What would a man quilter look like, I wondered?

"Silly. Just like any woman quilter would look like. Normal," Grama shrugged. So-called normal is always open to interpretation, I've found.

"I suppose," I said out loud before I realized it but he didn't seem to hear.

The man in the shop looked like, well, a fireman. He was middle-aged I guessed, receding hairline, tall and with broad shoulders but kinda filled out and comfortable-looking. There was a bulk to him that gave you the sense of confidence that he would be able to carry you out of a burning building with ease. Built for comfort, not speed, as Grama used to say. Sort of beat-up but friendly in a stray cat kind of way. Hobbes had jumped down from his windowseat to greet me on my entrance with a brief twining around my legs as usual, but when he saw the stranger he retreated to the cash desk where he kept a watchful eye from that elevated vantage point.

The man browsed around casually for a few minutes, touching a few things here and there. "You have a lovely store," he said, looking at me over a shelf. I thanked him in return. For some reason I was inordinately pleased and felt myself flush a little. By then he had wandered into the section of purple fabrics and picked out two bolts from the shelf. He carried them to the cutting table so I moved there also. Purple was a pretty safe choice for a man. I might have predicted that.

"I'll take . . ." he started to say as he laid the bolts down and then fumbled in his breast pocket, withdrawing a piece of paper which he consulted before finishing, "one and a quarter yards of each, please."

"Sure thing," I replied and smiled across the table at him as I reached out for the bolt. Our eyes met and lingered for that extra longer split-second of time, that excess of contact, than politeness decrees, and it unnerved me. He was too direct, yet he had such beautiful blue eyes I didn't want to look away. They were all twinkly and softened with crow's feet around them. It's always a man's eyes that get me. What is it, windows of the soul, they say?

I suddenly felt myself go all hot. Then, just as quickly, a carping little voice in me said, "Don't be silly," and I calmed right down. He's probably married or gay, I thought, and it reminded me of a cartoon I once saw about two women talking in a park. One says, "All the interesting men are either married or gay!" The other says, "That's ridiculous." The first one says, "I'll prove it to you," and calls out to a jogger passing by, "Hey you! In the blue shorts with the cute butt! Married or gay?" The man calls back, "Both!"

Besides, I don't have time for any of that, I lectured myself as I carefully cut his fabric. After so many years of dealing with men in a counselling capacity, I had grown used to keeping a professional distance from every one of them, even the otherwise attractive and available ones. "This is no different," I muttered under my breath.

"Excuse me?" he asked, looking up.

"Oh, nothing," I waved him off.

He hesitated, gazing at me for a long moment before looking back to consult his list again. "Do you have any, um, fusable interface?" he asked.

"Yes. I have Wunder-Under. Do you want a package? I also have it on a roll in strips if you like."

"Hmm." He hesitated again, staring off into a vacant space over my left shoulder. As I waited it gave me a polite chance to study his face again. He was definitely attractive. Tanned, strong jaw and cheekbones, a long nose and those seductive eyes. There were little red nicks where he had scraped his neck shaving.

"If you tell me what it's for I might be able to make a suggestion. What is your, um, wife going to do with it?" I asked, trying to keep my voice calm and professional but friendly. I checked his ring finger. No ring. No tan line where there could have been a ring. What had come over me! What was I thinking! Only prowling women in bars do that sort of thing, I thought in rebuke. "Oh, really?" asked Grama from her perch.

And what would Jennifer and Susan, or even Robbie, say about their mother being interested in a man? In a split second I knew the answer. Outgoing and bubbly Jennifer would say, go for it Mom! But sentimental and insecure Susan would say, Mom, how could you be disloyal to Daddy? My thoughtful and gentle son would simply shrug equably and say, whatever you want Mom. On average they were being no help at all.

The fireman looked me straight in the eye. Then waited for a long moment before slowly replying, "Oh. Hmm. Well, M'am I don't have a wife. It's, it's ah, for my . . . mother!" he exclaimed as if he was surprised by the answer himself. "Yes, my mother. She doesn't get out anymore, but she sure loves to make quilts. I pick things up for her, you know." He tried to shrug nonchalantly.

Yeah right, I thought. And my uncle's a ballet dancer. If you're a closet quilter, what else do you do in that closet, I wondered. I know guff when I hear it. Oh well, I sighed mentally, and wrote him off.

In the end he decided on a package of interface, then remembered to pick up some white cotton thread. I carried his "mother's" purchases to the cash register. He followed me, but when he reached the counter, Hobbes, who had crouched down in a pounce position, suddenly arched his back and spat with his clawless paws extended out, ready for weaponless attack.

"Hobbes!" I spoke sharply and put my hand against his chest, pushing him away. But Hobbes just retreated to the far corner standing his ground. "Scat, silly cat," I said in embarassment. Scat? I can't remember ever saying that to Hobbes before. Scat? What had come over me? But then Hobbes had never been so unfriendly before. If he doesn't like you, he usually just leaves the room in disdain. Maybe Hobbes knows guff too.

"I'm sorry," I apologized. "He never does that. And he has no claws anyway so he's completely harmless." Yeah, I thought, except for a full set of teeth.

The man laughed and said, "Sure. Like every Doberman owner says 'he never bites' just before ol' Brutus chews your face off!"

"I'm really sorry," I said again, reddening with embarrassment.

He just smiled and waved away my concern. "It's okay. No harm. Actually I really like cats." He looked at Hobbes and put his hand out, palm up, to make friends, but my guardcat would have nothing to do with him. "And they usually like me, too." Then he spoke directly to Hobbes, "I've saved a few of your pals from trees, remember!"

I smiled but Hobbes ignored the persuasion.

The man shrugged and handed me the money for his purchases. It was then that I noticed his hands. They were thick and strong and calloused. And they were heavily marked with several large patches of scar-tissue that were pulled taut and white between the dark tanned areas of unburned skin. I'd never seen a fireman's hands up close before and I wondered if it was a normal occupational hazard or if he had been in a terrible disaster. I hoped he didn't catch me staring at him.

"Come again," I smiled as I handed him his paper bag.

"Thank you Ma'am. I sure will," he replied, returning my smile. There were those amused blue eyes again, lingering. "See ya', Hobbes," he called over his shoulder. When he reached the door he turned and gave me a casual two-finger salute and then closed it carefully. Hobbes jumped down and followed him to the door, then returned to his aerie in the window.

As I stood watching the empty doorway, I twisted and twined my fingers in the gold chain around my neck. It holds the locket which Jack gave me on our tenth anniversary.

"Nice teeth," I heard Grama say after the fireman had gone. I saw her out of the corner of my eye. She was sitting on the window ledge petting Hobbes and grinning mischievously. Grama always had a thing about polished shoes and good teeth, saying that both denoted good breeding. "Nice teeth," she repeated.

I ignored her and turned to my busy-ness.

"Maybe it's time, honey," she commented about my earlier blush. It had been a long while since I'd had a decent date.

"It was just a hot flash," I rationalized.

"Yeah right," she replied archly.

"Go . . . a . . . way," I ordered as I busied myself tidying shelves once again. "Besides, you're just a figment of my imagination."

"Aggie, honey, you always say that when you're in denial," she replied but when I looked again, she had gone. "Good," I said to the air. Besides, for me it was always laughter in the eyes that was the deadly attraction.

I NEVER DID GO TO THE CABLE TV STATION. By Saturday afternoon, several customers had come into the shop and I had received half a dozen telephone calls. Amazingly, nine women signed up for the class. I had to explain that I didn't know what the lesson was going to be about or how much it would cost. If they would just turn up on the night I would let Jo handle it all. That didn't seem to bother anyone.

And when the next Tuesday night rolled around, eleven women showed up.

I made coffee for everyone. I thought it would relax us. In reality, I was the one who needed to relax. Someone asked me a question about shrinking fabric and my mind went blank. I couldn't answer. It would have been easier if they'd needed their head shrunk, so to speak. That was a more familiar line of work. I hoped everyone would be pleased with the class but I felt out of control. The women milled around the shop and commented favorably. A good sign.

Jo came dashing in right at seven o'clock just as the class was supposed to start. It had been a cool, rainy day and that night she was wearing a pair of white chinos and a sleeveless multi-pock-eted photographer's vest over a navy cableknit sweater. She looked as if she belonged on the beach at Cape Cod or on a safari in Africa. I wondered what she did in her real life—when she wasn't popping in and out of my shop.

The first thing she did was ask everyone to introduce themselves around the table and say what they knew about quilting and what they wanted to learn. It certainly was a mixed group. A couple of the women owned their own quilt frames and had either used them, or not. Some had quilted before, some had not. Some knew Jo already, some didn't. Some were old, some young. Everyone had a different story to tell: my aunt quilted; I just want to save money and make a co-ordinated bedspread to match my newly decorated bedroom; I'm looking for a creative outlet; I've done every other craft and now I'm "doing" quilting. One woman laughed as she admitted that she couldn't stop once she'd started quilting nine years ago! There were as many motives as there were quilters. What a mess, I thought in dismay, mentally trying to organize classes. There would have to be at least three different classes to accommodate all the skill levels. And if this was the limit of the town's interest, then how would I fill a Saturday class too? I felt distressed.

None of this seemed to bother Jo. Everyone was friendly and even the newcomers quickly relaxed. Finally, after introducing herself, Jo told us to gather around because she wanted to tell us a story. She called it a quilting folk tale. It seemed like a funny beginning, but was in keeping with everything else she did.

"Once upon a time," she began. "in a far away kingdom there lived a poor farmer. He had a good wife who worked very hard, and they had a beautiful daughter called Able. One year the crop was very poor. There would be little to eat come Winter and Able's mother secretly gave her meager portions of food to Able. 'Mother you are so thin. You must eat,' cried Able, seeing her mother's empty plate. But Mother demured, saying, 'I already ate, dear one. Besides, I am filled up completely when I see how beautiful you have grown.'

"As cold weather approached, every night after the work was done and everyone was asleep Able's mother sewed a special quilt for Able. Her fingers ached from the careful stitching, her eyes swam from the poor candle light and she shivered with cold, but she would not stop. The quilt must be finished before . . ." Jo drew a breath.

"Oh, oh. She's going to die!" a woman in a red sweater exclaimed in apprehension.

"Stop interrupting," someone chided.

"No. No. It's alright," assured Jo. "Heckling is an old tradition among storytellers. It's just anticipation and it shows the teller that you're involved in the story."

Jo continued. "But soon the cold weather came and Able's mother lay dying. She called her daughter to her bedside. Able was distraught and cried, 'Mother, you mustn't leave us! What will become of us!' 'Don't worry, darling daughter. Under my bed you will find a box and in it is a quilt I made for you. It's a special quilt that will look after you. Keep it with you always and I will be there with you.' And saying that, Able's mother drew her last breath and drifted away from her earthy troubles.

"From that night on Able slept beneath the quilt. Before she fell asleep she would ask the quilt to keep her safe, and make tomorrow a better day. No matter how cold life was, she was warmed by the quilt.

"When Able was grown, because she was so poor she had no dowry or hopes of marrying well. Her father wanted her to be independent and not marry a farmer like himself so he sent Able to the village to be a handmaid to the Manor."

"I know, she marries the son of the Manor and lives happily ever after," one woman interrupted.

"No. Not at all. Gather round, my dears and listen," Jo continued as if she were a Medieval troubador. "All the other household help laughed at Able and her naive ways, her simple dress, and especially her silly old dull quilt. Dull? How could they call her wonderful quilt dull, she wondered. But then she saw the beautiful silk comforters on the lord of the Manor's bed, and for the first time she saw how homely her lowly homespun quilt was. She was ashamed and sad.

"One day, a fire broke out in the Manor kitchen and there was great panic. The lord of the Manor ran here and there and shouted orders, to get buckets of water, to beat back the flames and to have the servants save his precious possessions. The men ran to stop the fire. The women ran to save the gold plate and crystal. But Able ran upstairs to her small attic room to save her mother's quilt. 'You can't go up there,' they yelled at her. 'I must!' she cried and off she stumbled through the black smoke. Her head knew the quilt was ugly and worthless but her heart knew it was priceless.

"The fire could not be stopped. The Manor could not be saved. The lord lost much that he prized and was angry that Able had not helped him save his gold and crystal. He sent her away.

"She sat for a long time by the roadside hugging her quilt and crying. But as luck would have it, a traveling merchant stopped and took her to the big city, and into his household. She met the honest merchant's son. And after some time passed they planned to wed. The young man had a gentle heart and he ingeniously suggested to Able that she keep her mother's quilt but that she make a beautiful new top and use her mother's quilt to line their wedding quilt. She loved him all the more passionately for his tenderness.

"Even though her new friends in the City, the other young merchants' brides, admired her lovely new quilt and shared her joy in her wedding, only Able knew her mother's old beloved quilt was there inside to keep her safe and warm."

"And they lived happily ever after," the woman in the red sweater suggested.

"And they lived happily ever after," Jo agreed.

"What an interesting story," someone said.

"What does it mean?" another woman asked.

"I think it means, even an ugly old quilt is valuable," interjected one newcomer. "So perhaps even someone inexperienced like me can make something worthwhile."

Jo nodded. "That's why her name was Able."

"I get it! Folk stories usually tell some moral and the characters are supposed to be symbolic. So everyone is Able, and able, small a," someone analyzed.

Jo nodded again. "People think that folk stories come *from* the folk, but actually folk stories and fairy tales are a way of communicating deep ideas and profound lessons *to* the folk, disguised as amusing or simple anecdotes. It's an ancient tradition. Think of the parables in the Bible."

Then a younger woman spoke and the room grew quiet for a minute.

"But on another level, it was her mother's quilt that took care of her—because she would never let go of it no matter what. She saved it in the face of criticism from others and from the fire and she even lost her job over it. That could mean that we have to value the treasures of the past, of our mothers," she commented.

"And if we do, we can connect to our spiritual mothers, who will protect us, through quilting, or through all our creative acts," said an experienced quilter.

Jo nodded.

"Perhaps it means something different to everyone, just as quilting means different things to different people," said a quiet woman who hadn't spoken until then.

"Yes. Yes. Yes." Jo smiled with satisfaction and clapped her hands.

Everyone had taken what she needed from the story. Jo's fairy tale seemed to please and in some strange way to energize the group. It was as if the story gave everyone the permission they needed to be different, and yet still be okay. It was an ingenious beginning to the class. I admired Jo's unusual approach.

In the end there was a mellow glow to the gathering as we said goodnight. Jo sent everyone home with instructions. The experienced quilters were to bring their works in progress to the next class. The new quilters were to come back sometime this week and shop for a pattern they liked and pick out fabric. I was to help them with their choices—within their budgets, I was warned good-humoredly. Everyone would pay six dollars a week—which Jo and I would split. That seemed like a fair beginning.

After closing the shop I complimented Jo on her unorthodox teaching style. It seemed this wasn't going to be your usual six or ten week course in quilting. This was more of an endless quilt-in. And potential chaos, I worried. "How can you teach everyone at the same time?" I asked her. "They are all so dissimilar."

Jo explained. "My grandmother taught school in a one room schoolhouse. How did she, and all the other teachers in her day, do it? Same thing," she shrugged. "You see, here's the thing about creativity and teaching everyone all together: there is no 'grade one' creativity, 'grade two' creativity, 'grade three' creativity, and so on. There is just creativity. *Techniques* have grades of skill; creativity does not. Any technique can be taught in five minutes of demonstration. What follows is just time for practising the skill. It doesn't need hand-holding or nurture. All it needs is time and space for the repetitive practise. It's the *creativity* which needs nurturing, mentoring and a supportive environment to grow in. I just happen to think that it's easier to nurture creativity in a group setting.

"Life is never doled out in simple one-thing-at-a-time install-ments. Life is all mixed up together. At any point in time, there are things you are good and proficient at, and things you are new and awkward at. And that's the way it's supposed to be. There's always someone better at something than you are, and someone worse. For me it would be harder to try to separate everyone into different skill levels where they supposedly 'belong.'"

"That's not a very traditional approach," I pointed out. I could agree with her theoretically but I suggested that her method would have difficulty in practise.

"That's not my problem," she replied impatiently. "That's the problem with schools today. I'm probably old-fashioned but I think that's how it should still be in classrooms. In the old way, the older students helped younger ones to learn the basics. And the junior students taught the senior ones too—to keep their eyes open and fresh and not to assume they knew everything. I've seen some exciting quilts produced by beginners who weren't afraid to say 'why can't I put this fabric next to that?' That way we can all learn together."

"Well, I see what you mean," I said. "It bothers me the way we put everyone in competition with each other instead of teaching students to cooperate and help each other. We teach that to col-laborate on results is called cheating! I read somewhere that in Asia to cheat is to *not* help your neighbor! They teach that everyone is better off, individually and as a community, when we help one another. For them it isn't about our American values of hell-bent-for-leather individualism and independence. It's about collaboration and harmony."

"Now there's a truly different mindset for you," Jo commented. "What would our society be like if we all worked cooperatively, instead of competing?"

I thought about women quilting together.

"The quilting bee," I said, and Jo nodded, acknowledging the metaphor of pioneer women working together on one quilt. At a quilting bee, every woman invests her best stitches in the quilts of other women because she knows they will invest their best stitches in her quilt in turn.

"That's what is great about quilt classes," Jo continued. "We all produce better work when we support, encourage and help one another. You see, I'm not the only one who has anything to teach here. I'm really only responsible for the inspiration and continued motivation."

"How can you help people let ideas jump out of their subconscious, or have just the right fabric 'jump out of their stash?'" I asked.

"Oh, that's easy," she replied with a mischievous grin. "Believe it or not, most people want to be creative. *Women* want to be creative. All they need is the *permission* to try, and the *space* to do it in. After that they'll do all the rest by following their instincts or intuition!"

"Shouldn't they just give themselves permission?" As soon as I said it I knew it was a stupid question. I knew better than that. We're always looking to other people for validation in life.

"Of course, but there are so many things that happen to us that take away our creative spirits—from the very first time we tell a child to color between the lines, or that the sun is always yellow, the leaves are green and the sky is blue. Even when we know it isn't true, by the time we grow up we don't know how to be free anymore. Ask any kindergarten class if they can draw and the resounding answer is 'Yes!' Ask them if they can sing, and they are more than eager to show you what they can do. Even if they are a little off key, they sing with gusto because no one has convinced them yet that they can't sing, or draw. No one has taken away their joy of singing, their joy of doing.

"We're so programmed to seek approval and permission from others that that's where we have to receive it first—from others—before we learn to give it to ourselves."

It was an interesting perspective on creativity. I wondered if Grama had ever thought of her quilting that way. Jo reminded me so much of Grama. I could imagine the two of them talking together, rapid fire, finishing each other's sentences like long-time friends often do. Talking with Jo was like talking with a colleague, one I'd known for years. There was meat to her. She didn't strike me as the kind of woman who sat around discussing recipes or floorwax.

"You know a lot about teaching. Were you ever a teacher?" I asked as we sat talking toward midnight, drinking cups of tea. Ironically, it was the longest conversation I would ever have with Jo.

"No, but you could say that teaching was always part of my business life," she explained as she told me her story. "A long time ago . . ." She laughed. "It sounds like another fairy tale, doesn't it? I was left a widow with a young son to raise. I had to work, so I sold furniture at a department store—that's where I learned about customer service and retailing. But I also had an interest in health, since my son, Jeremy, had allergies. So I started making cleansers and soaps in my kitchen at night. They had all-natural ingredients so my son could use them.

"Friends started asking for them, and then buying them, and soon I had a small kitchen-counter business—that's where I learned about sales, and disappointments and how not to take rejection personally. That old brown and green kitchen was the start of Jo Belle Products." She laughed again. "Everyone thought I chose the company colors to reflect my 'environmentally friendly' products. Actually it was just the colors in my kitchen!"

"I had no idea! You're Jo of Jo Belle! Grama used your hand soap for years." I was open-mouthed in admiration. "But good grief, Jo, you must have bags of money, why on earth do you live in Clareville!" I exclaimed, rudely interrupting her story. It occurred to me that she certainly didn't need the money from the quilt class. Obviously she was doing it for love, not money.

Jo smiled. "Well yes, I suppose I'm comfortable. But after all I have to live somewhere. Why do you live here?"

"Because I was tired of the city. I thought it would be more peaceful here. I like small towns. Somehow they seem friendlier and more . . . I don't know, what's the word? Human? And this was my late husband's hometown, so I feel like it's home to me, too."

Jo smiled again. "It's always been home to me too. I thought about moving away years ago but I decided that having money wasn't about an expensive condo at an exclusive address. In any event," she continued, "by the time Jeremy had grown up my night business had taken over my daytime and I had to get serious. They told me I was too old to have a 'real' business. Despite the nay-sayers I ended up with a staff and a production line— that's where I learned about so-called big business. Eventually I had to expand and I went to the bank for funding—"

"And that's where you learned about women and banks!" I anticipated and she nodded. "I know all about that. Even though statistics prove women are more reliable in repaying small business loans, and that women work harder and longer at their businesses, and more often succeed at those small businesses, banks still don't want to loan money to a woman without her husband's signature, and his income backing it up. It's so unfair!"

Jo nodded again. "Fortunately I'm retired from all that now. My son runs the business day-to-day although I usually still attend Board meetings. The teaching you asked about was the result of having to teach customers about my products and about natural health care before it was popular to do so. I taught sales techniques to my staff, and I even taught bank managers about small businesses and *women* in business."

"Well, you could probably teach me, if you want. There's a lot I need to know," I said.

Then I told Jo about Jennifer and Robbie and Susan. And Grama. I told her about leaving the city to come here and about how I had set out optimistically with just a little trepidation but how the scale had begun to tip the other way, that fears were overwhelming me, that I was beginning to doubt myself and my decision. I don't know why I unburdened myself but we were getting to know each other and she was a patient listener.

"Jo, I'm feeling really lost," I said. "It's okay that the kids are grown up and don't need me as much and I've lost my primary role of mother-guidance counsellor. That's all right. But for the first time in years in my professional life I really don't know what I'm doing, or what I'm supposed to do. Sometimes I feel free and sometimes like I'm in chains. I feel disoriented. I haven't felt like this since I was twenty."

"You're not lost, Aggie," Jo replied reassuringly. She patted the table. "You're right here, where you're supposed to be. In order to be lost you have to want to be someplace else. Do you want to be some other *specific* place?"

I shook my head.

"No. Right. Then you're not lost. You're just at a crossroads, that's all. You'll be okay once you decide which direction you're headed. Don't pretend to know exactly where you're going. If you know where you're going, it means you've probably already been there, and you will wind up right back where you came from."

That seemed to make some sort of circular sense. "But wasn't it the Cheshire Cat in *Alice in Wonderland* who said, 'If you don't know where you are going, it doesn't matter what road you take?'" I laughed.

"I think it may have been the caterpillar on the toadstool," Jo smiled. "What he *should* have said is, 'It doesn't matter what road you take because the paradox is, you'll end up there anyway.'"

"Oh dear. That sounds even more enigmatic. Are you going to disappear now, like a genie in a puff of smoke, or slowly dissolve leaving your grin behind, like the Cheshire Cat?" I laughed. "So, you're saying 'all roads lead to Rome,' right?"

"No. All roads lead to *home*," she corrected. "Spiritual home."

"Ah so," I nodded, as if I understood. This would take some thinking.

I was reminded of a story about the astronaut, Jim Lovell, I told Jo. I suppose everyone who was alive at the time of the first trip to the moon was affected by that journey. It was a journey we all took together. You went out there, you came back, and you were transformed by the experience. I read every newspaper account about the brave new astronauts. I listened to Walter Cronkite each night and I died a little death with the men on Apollo 5.

Most of all I remember a story about what happened to Jim Lovell when he was a young fighter pilot flying back from a training mission over the Pacific Ocean. It was night, pitch dark, and he was lost. His radar was jammed, and when he flipped on the interior map light in his cockpit all the interior lights blew out. He was in total darkness. High clouds obscured the stars he could have navigated by. He had no way to see his path home. Then suddenly he looked down and spotted a trail of green phosphorescence in the water. It was the algae which had been stirred up by a large ship, his aircraft carrier. All he had to do was follow the trail of green algae to home. "So, even in the darkest, sightless night," I told Jo, "You never know what trail will lead you home. And sometimes you have to *be* in total darkness before you're able to see the faint light guiding you home."

Jo and I were both quiet for a few moments as we thought about what it means to search for and find home.

Then tactfully and lightly changing the subject, Jo said she was pleased that I, too, had joined the class and was working on a quilt.

"You can't be in the business and not be a quilter yourself. That's the first thing you need to know. If you're not passionate about what you're doing, your customers will sense it as a lack of commitment and they'll be unconnected. There are lots of tools and techniques to learn about quilting, but the only thing I cannot teach is passion. Everyone has to go out and find their own passion. 'Follow your bliss' as Joseph Campbell used to say. He studied all the world's mythologies and religions and it was a favorite theme of his that everyone achieves wisdom, or some sort of state of grace by doing whatever they are passionate about. According to him, it's the only way to fulfil your true destiny. If you are passionate and involved with what you do, a lot of other things fall into place. When you have passion everything else is just mechanics. When you come up against obstacles, if you have passion, you'll find creative ways around the problem.

"Look, I don't know why you're in Clareville either," Jo continued, "But I know that in your role as quilt shop owner you are a spiritual leader of women in the community. You are here to provide the physical space and materials, and more importantly, the psychic space which gives women the freedom to express themselves creatively, from the heart, without fear and without criticism."

Then she laughed. "Wow! That sounds heavy, doesn't it? That'll probably scare you out of town for good!" I nodded vigorously. "It's okay though. You're also allowed to make money and have fun at the same time, you know," she reassured me.

"Thanks for that," I smiled. "What you say reminds me of something Grama once told me about finding our higher purpose. She said that the honeybee goes to a flower seeking nectar, and in the process carries away pollen to another flower. Sometimes we think our purpose is one thing, like making honey. Or money. Our true purpose may be deeper and less visible, like cross-pollinating flowers. Or perhaps in my case, germinating creativity. So I think I understand what you're saying."

"Good example," Jo replied. "People spend too much time thinking about money. They worry about how to get it and then how to keep it. It's my experience that the best way to make a bad decision is to base it on money. People worry about how to acquire 'stuff' and then they're afraid they're going to lose their 'stuff,' instead of thinking 'I will be the best possible mother I can be,' or 'I will be the best quilt shop owner I can be.' You have to think about what you can do in life, not what you will gain in terms of money."

"That's true," I said, "but I don't think you can think about those higher purpose things much. It stops you from living each day. If you think about the hidden dimension to life excessively you end up trying to catch your own shadow. You're so busy watching yourself, you miss out seeing life go by. Maybe we can't see our own purpose. The very act of looking at it, of being self-conscious, changes it. We simply have to act on faith that we are fulfilling a higher purpose. That's what keeps me going."

"Hmm. Interesting," Jo commented. "Sounds like your Grama would have been a wonderful Wombat."

"A what?" I laughed. "A wombat?" Images of a furry animal with fangs jumped into my mind.

"We have a local Women's Business Association, the Clareville WBA. That's the official title of the whole group. But there are a number of us, a sort of subgroup, and we call ourselves Wombats: Women of Menopause Business Association and Terrorist Society!" Jo explained. I laughed at the acronym.

"I guess you could say we're a group of opinionated women who've grown too old to care what others think. There's a wonderful power and freedom that comes with middle and old age. Aging doesn't have to be a time of loss. It can be a time of gaining, of gaining wisdom."

She paused. "We take on projects that other people are too busy, or too complacent to get involved in. We raised funds for a CAT Scan machine at the hospital. We got traffic lights installed at the intersection of Carson and Pine Ridge where there were too many accidents. We also talked the Library Board into establishing a Women's Studies section."

I laughed again. "Sounds like the right kind of place for me. I think it was menopause madness that got me into this business in the first place. Have you chained yourselves to any buildings lately?"

"No, but there are a few male chauvinists in this town we'd like to chain up. You haven't met Little Al Junior yet, have you?"

"No. Who's he?"

"Uncle Al Senior's son," she replied as if that were an explanation. I must have looked blank. "You know, 'Uncle Al.' Al Brown, used car salesman turned politician. The town mayor."

"Oh," I nodded finally in recognition.

"His son's a class A jerk. Half a yard short of a bolt, if you ask me. Wait til you see," she warned. "He used to be such a promising young man. . . ."

She kept talking but I had stopped listening. I was thinking about the Wombats, and picturing a troop of little old grey-haired ladies in battle fatigues, brandishing garden trowels and soup ladles, yelling "Geritol" as they swooped into action. Grama definitely would have fitted in. It was terribly late by then and I guess I was getting silly.

". . . And that's why Little Al presents a problem," Jo concluded as I tuned back into what she was saying. She drained the last of her tea, stretched and stood up to leave.

Shortly afterwords, we finally said goodnight. I told Jo I was looking forward to meeting the Wombats, and I truly was.

It was too late and I was too tired that evening to start working on my second quilt block but two days later I again retreated to the calm pool of light over the cutting table in the darkened shop to put my feelings into fabric. My second block is called *Crossroads*. That's where I was in life. I had left the old, but the new hadn't defined itself clearly yet. I had gone this far on a leap of faith. I recalled what Grama said to me when Jack died and I was wondering how I would carry on without him with three children to raise. Beyond feeling grief, I was scared near to death myself. Grama had put her arm around my shoulder to console me. She was a head shorter but at the time I felt so small and helpless that she seemed taller than I was, and certainly stronger. She had lost a husband and then she had lost a son.

"Courage is simply a decision you make at crossroads," she said.

There I was at crossroads again, and feeling overwhelmed. But all I have to do is make each decision one by one, I reminded myself. My *Crossroads* block would remind me to have courage and know that I'm not lost. Being at a crossroads can be an opportunity for renewed creativity. But only if we fearlessly say "yes" to the open door and step across the threshold. There is probably challenge on the other side, and maybe also confusion and chaos, but that is where the crossroads lead.

"Trouble? Life is trouble. Only death is no trouble," Zorba said in the movie *Zorba, the Greek*.

I liked the idea of a *Crossroads* block because a road implies a journey, travel from one place to another. Maybe my quilt would become a roadmap of where I'm going, or at least a travel diary of where I've been. The pieces of a *Crossroads* block form a criss-cross of pathways, some that lead in and out of the block, some which go around in circles, interlocking with other blocks. When we say "yes" we step onto one of those interlocking paths in life. Despite the difficulty and the chaos, the path is meant to be expansive and joyous. It's only when we deny the inner urges because we are afraid, that our lives become miserable and small, that our destinations become limited.

I found some interesting scraps in Grama's stash. I had forgotten about one fabric—a colorful children's print. The kind of design that makes you smile just to look at it. It has little cartoon trains and airplanes and cars on it—from the decade when it was considered only a boy's print. Grama made it into pajamas for Robbie when he was a baby. By cutting it carefully I was able to have the little vehicles traveling up and down the crossed roads. I figured I might as well keep a sense of humor while I find my way. If I'm going to look back at this time from somewhere down the road and laugh, I may as well laugh now.

Laughter keeps our lives open and expanding.

THREE

Kansas Trouble

IN THE END I FOUND OUT who Little Al Junior was sooner than I expected, or would have wanted. In spite of my misgivings the shop had done well and I found an assistant, Joyce, to help out. She was one of the enthusiastic newcomers who had attended the quilt class and needed a part-time job. A week later, I had just finished my first set of accounts and was feeling pretty pleased with myself. Not with the numbers themselves, they could stand to be a lot better, but with the fact that I had actually balanced the books. Jo stopped by the shop wearing a conservative blue crepe suit and lots of diamond jewelry. It was the kind of outfit you wear to impress your future mother-in-law or a bank manager. It struck me that I had not seen Jo dressed in the same style twice. It was like watching a chameleon.

"It's Wednesday. Are you ready for the meeting tonight?" she asked.

"What meeting? I thought the Wombats met every other Thursday," I replied, putting the accounting books away.

"The town meeting, of course," she said curtly.

"Oh that. I saw the flyer but haven't had time to read it. I'm not much interested in politics," I said.

"Well! You'd better be, lady!" she said huffily.

Now this was one thing she was not going to drag me into, I decided. I had quite enough on my plate already. I'm not going to any boring old town meeting, I thought to myself.

"How can you not be interested? They're going to tear down the town square and this row of shops with it," she said.

I stared at her in disbelief.

"What!" I spluttered, stunned. "What do you mean!"

47

"They're going to tear down the town square and this row of shops with it," she repeated irritably. "Which part of that didn't you understand?"

"Oh no. They can't do that. This is my business. This is my home! They can't do that!" I declared.

"Exactly. I'll see you there at eight o'clock," she said and left.

"Wait!" I called but she had disappeared.

In a panic I rummaged through the basket of unread mail. I found the notice and, sure enough, it contained some suspiciously small and evil-looking legal terms that basically, and rather unemotionally considering the circumstances, stated that I-dear-occupant was about to be expropriated. There was a proposal to be put before Council to construct a modern shopping center and, horrors, a parking lot in the town square. I was devastated! They might as well be putting a highway through my livingroom. In essence that's exactly what they were doing. I felt sick. I could lose my store. I could lose everything. I blanched at the thought. I was in a tailspin. Clareville suddenly stopped being my sleepy green haven.

Then I got angry and a hot pink flush crept up my neck.

It occurred to me: what else was lurking unread in the mail! So I grabbed the pile and read every line of every single piece of paper. It *was* worse than I thought. There was a notice from the Fire Marshall, who doubles as the Town Clerk, declaring that my building didn't meet fire safety standards and would require the following work, *aka* money, to bring it up to snuff. I had already met this particular obnoxious Uriah Heap official when I applied for my business license. I smelled a rat. Yellow spots began to pop in front of my eyes. I wondered if he just happened to have a brother in the fire safety or renovation business. Then I found a letter from the bank manager politely asking me to come in to discuss the refinancing of my business loan. I had just financed it, I didn't need to *re*-finance it. I knew what that meant, and now I smelled the big rotten cheese that all the rats were after. All of a sudden Clareville had become "the town from Hell!" Now I was really seeing red.

I went into a flap for the rest of the afternoon. I paced the shop, waving my arms, rhetorically entreating the Goddess of Irony to explain, "Why me!" But the Gods weren't answering. I was the picture of frantic angst and apoplectic purple. I had already been a rainbow of emotions but there were still several hours to go before the bomb was about to hit, at the town meeting.

Suddenly my mettle was up. I might have been asleep before but I was wide awake then!

I was in a brown funk by the time I arrived at the monthly Council meeting that evening. The hall was already filling up. Apparently, the shopping center had been common knowledge for quite some time. The initial rumors were confirmed and the town had been discussing it at length, opposing lines were being drawn. I seemed to be the only one with my head in the sand. Perhaps because I was a newcomer, no one thought to talk to me about it. Perhaps that was what Jo had been talking about the night she mentioned Little Al Junior and the Wombats. And perhaps I should have read my mail.

I thought about the former owners of my shop and imagined them sitting contently, far away in Georgia, sipping peach cocktails and eating pecan pie. Not all the swampland that gets sold is in Florida, I decided.

I was charging down the aisle toward a seat in the front row when Jo grabbed my arm and hauled me to a back row seat. "Shh," she shushed me as I started to blurt out my anger. "We're here to reconnoitre, not to engage in battle," she explained. "This is just a preliminary meeting. Nothing will be decided tonight. We need to see who stands where. Better to have two ears than one voice. Keep your mouth shut and your eyes open," she said tersely as she pulled me into a seat.

I was amazed at her presence of mind under the circumstances. But then again, this wasn't threatening her directly. Her business was in her head, not on Main Street. Her concern was aesthetic, or historic, not economic.

But Jo was right, of course. Except for the highly-charged emotional atmosphere in the Councilroom, it appeared to be a very boring business-as-usual meeting. I sat nervously fingering my locket, calling on Jack's presence to reassure myself, as Mayor Al Brown presided over the meeting with easy familiarity, handling the humdrum town business in a professional and speedy manner. Although he was dressed in a sober blue suit and wore a Mickey Mouse tie with matching suspenders, and despite my state of mind, I was pretty impressed. And it gave me a chance to stop hyperventilating.

My assistant, Joyce, had filled me in on the town Council. "Uncle Al" Brown had become one of the town's leading lights from humble beginnings. He started life as "a tin man," a traveling aluminium siding salesman, who graduated to used cars when he decided to "settle down," and finally ended up owning the only new car dealership in town. He was then a successful and respectable businessman. And although he was still the gregarious and affable personality from his earlier traveling salesman days, for the most part everyone agreed that he was basically honest, and that he always kept his word. It was just hard to get his word out of him. Like all good salesmen, he wanted to please people. His customers, the Council, and the townspeople. That was also his great flaw. He had an overwhelming need to be liked, and in an earnest endeavor to please everyone he tended to sit on the fence whenever a decision was called for. Unlike P. T. Barnum he didn't seem to realize that you can't please all the people all the time. Whenever possible he let others make the decisions. That way he could never be held responsible for the outcome. I suppose he never actually "sold" a lemon but a lot of his customers must have "bought" one anyway.

He had apparently been able to import a classy wife from an old patrician family in Boston who managed to tone down his suits, but he was never able to outlive his "Uncle Al" used car salesman name. He and his wife produced one son, Little Al Junior. According to Joyce, Al Senior's biggest mistake was in introducing Al Junior to two things: a career in sales, and a real estate license.

It was Little Al Junior who was spearheading the redevelopment project. As a young man in the real estate business, he had purchased several rental properties on the town square as an investment. Somewhere along the line he cooked up the plan to buy all the land and redevelop it as an intown shopping complex. Since then he had been quietly acquiring other properties around the town square. By offering slightly more than the market value of the property he had convinced some of the owners to sell and now he owned half the block where I lived. He stood to earn mega-bucks on the redevelopment and he needed Council's support to rezone the parkland and make it happen. If Council approved his plan, the remaining properties would be expropriated, in effect bought at a lower market value based on the tax rate. And of course that would not take anyone's inventory or leasehold improvements into account.

It was a risky but shrewd business venture. I suspected there was something of the eternal son-outdoing-his-father's-success in the story somewhere. Maybe it would help if everyone stopped calling him *Little* Al Junior, I thought.

The only time Mayor Brown looked uncomfortable was when his son stood up to present the proposal. Al Junior was a younger version of his father, *sans* wacky tie. He was of medium height and medium build, and he wore a beautifully-tailored gray suit, crisp white shirt and blue tie. His face was marred only by a feeble attempt at a moustache.

Naturally, Al Junior's rationale sounded perfectly... well, rational. He even managed to make it appear as if he was doing the town a favor and that he was being altruistic after all. He argued that if he, a local good ole' boy, didn't do it, some outside developer or super chainstore would build a megamall outside town and that would be the end of the downtown shopping district. This was already happening across the United States, he pointed out. It was true. The spectre of that possibility brought visible chills to the hearts of the merchants on the square. When I bought the shop I never realized that the old town center was such a problem. I knew that traffic was congested and there were few convenient places to park, but I assumed that this was a normal part of doing business in a small town. I thought the old town had a quaint charm about it, albeit in a sleepy sort of way. The image of my pleasant little greenspace being turned into a parking lot surrounded by a chain link fence drove a cold dagger into my heart.

Al Junior's plan was supposed to bring higher tax dollars to the town and revitalize the economy. The reality was likely to put the downtown merchants out of business anyway because they wouldn't receive full value for their property, and then wouldn't be able to afford the higher rents in the new complex. We would end up with a bunch of out-of-town franchises and expensive boutiques along with our extra parking spaces. Hamburger palaces and superstores didn't fit with my vision of Clareville.

For some reason the old movie *The Rainmaker* kept flashing through my mind. It starred Burt Lancaster as a traveling con man who arrives in a small farm town during a drought and convinces an aging farmer, his three sons, and eventually even his highly dubious daughter, played by Katharine Hepburn, that if they banged on a huge drum it would cause rain, but only if they *believed* strongly enough. We, too, were being sold a promise of rain to cure the town's drought. And by the smiles on the nodding faces, there was a lot of agreement. These people would buy snake oil, I was sure. I had a terrible sinking feeling in my stomach.

But as Jo predicted, the motion was quickly tabled for two months until the next Council meeting, after the Summer recess—swept under the rug, I thought—and they went on with other business. And suddenly it was over. An anticlimax. I'd come to fight. I'd come for justice. I was a bag of mostly hot air with nowhere to go! I bit my locket to keep from screaming.

"Frank Dempsey looked pleased. He's probably in favor of the proposal. That's bad news. He has influence in town," Jo nudged me. I knew that Frank was one of the Councillors.

"I didn't see," I said.

"The guy, third row, second from right, in the expensive suit." Jo pointed with her nose.

I scanned the crowd but came to a dead stop when I saw the fireman from my quilt shop. He was looking right at me smiling. He nodded and grinned broadly when he caught my eye. "Who is he?" I wondered aloud, looking away again.

"Betcha he's one of Little Al's redevelopment buddies from the city."

That wasn't who I meant. "I didn't see," I muttered. She looked at me sternly. I shrugged. Since I can't recognize half the town people yet, how could she expect me to recognize a stranger?

"What do you think about Rita Appleton? She was smiling. She's known the Browns for years. I think she might support it," Jo said. She was referring to another Councillor.

"Gee. I don't know. I was watching Little Al," I apologized.

"What for? We *know* where he stands!" She shook her head at me.

"Sorry, boss." I felt stupid.

"We probably can't change the mind of anyone who wants this thing to pass. But we may be able to influence anyone who's undecided. And we can certainly support and reinforce anyone who opposes the proposal. So, we need to know who's in cahoots with him," Jo pointed out.

"*Cahoots*," I repeated. "I like that word. Do you think it's a plot, too?" I asked innocently.

"If it isn't, it will be," she nodded. "Well, we've got work to do. See you!" She disappeared. As usual. I was getting used to that.

After the meeting, it was a long sad journey home to Grama's Quilt Shop. Home. I looked in the darkened shop window and saw Hobbes peacefully curled up in the window, content and secure. My own reflection was superimposed ghostlike over his sleeping form. I pressed my fevered forehead to the cool glass. It may not be home for much longer, puss, I thought unhappily. I pictured myself as a homeless baglady with Hobbes and a dozen bolts of cloth loaded into a rusty shopping cart.

Then I got angry again. I will not let this happen, I mentally promised Hobbes. I straightened up and strengthened my resolve. I will not let this happen, I promised myself.

But as I slowly climbed the back stairs to my apartment, I said a small prayer.

AFTER THE UNSATISFYING TOWN MEETING I went to bed and had a terrible dream that night. I was in the tornado scene from *The Wizard of Oz*. Black clouds were swirled around me, the wind roared in my ears. Little Al Junior was riding the Wicked Witch's bicycle while Hobbes, our poor terrified cat, struggled to get out of the basket. Bolts of fabric and scissors and spools of thread were blowing up all around me. Either the world was spiralling upward or I was falling into a deep hole, tumbling around and around. Jo flew past me sitting cross-legged yoga-style on a frayed old quilt. She smiled and waved as she went by. I tried to call her back but she just kept waving and smiling until she disappeared piece by piece like the Cheshire Cat. All that was left was her waving hand.

When I woke up in the middle of the night, Hobbes was purring in my ear. Up close his breath was like the roaring tornado. He was his usual innocent happy self. Reluctantly, I got up and went downstairs to shake the dream out of my head. I flipped on the one light over the cutting table and sat down glumly. My normally cheerful rainbow of fabrics lay hidden in the gloom beyond the circle of light.

There had to be a quilt pattern to symbolize, and hopefully exorcise, this latest nightmare episode in my Clareville adventure, I decided. I don't know why it suddenly seemed so important to record those events, even the disastrous ones, in my quilt. Maybe focussing outward on an easy task like sewing would keep me from falling into despair. There was a good chance I could lose the shop, and then where would I be? I pulled out a pattern book and flipped desultorily through the pages, looking for my third quilt block.

I found it right away: the *Kansas Troubles* pattern. Another traditional design from pioneer days. I guess nothing changes: there's trouble in every generation.

Hobbes had followed me and sat casually washing his paws on the cutting table. Nothing bothers cats except an empty food bowl. "That's it, Toto, we're definitely not in Kansas anymore!" I quoted to him. He interrupted his wash and "brrr-upped" curiously so I showed him the pattern, and rubbed his waiting ears.

The Kansas Troubles pattern has four angular "spokes" which whirl around the block. Each snarly, barbed spoke looks like a spiky windmill, or like abstract black clouds flying off in every direction— just like a tornado. And I have the perfect fabric, I thought. Upstairs was a swatch of muddy brown cotton with ugly black swirls on it. I figured there must be a place even for homely fabrics, so that one would be just right for my Kansas tornado. It seemed my pleasant Clareville garden was being ripped apart by an evil wind. I'll make the background green like the sprouts of my new business, I thought, and like the trees in the park, around which the terrible, threatening dust devils would blow.

"My quilt blocks have taken a depressing downward turn," I observed to Toto-Hobbes.

Sometimes the crossroad we step onto turns out to be the narrow track of a rollercoaster. And when that rollercoaster slowly crawls uphill to the top we don't always see what's coming on the other side—a sudden and scary descent. By the time it happens, all you can do is hold on until you hit bottom again. Having said yes to the freefall bungee jump of life, I found that the ground was now rushing up toward me. I hope it stops soon, I prayed. It was already too late to get off. I had already made my emotional and financial commitment to the shop and, indirectly, to Clareville.

At least I wasn't confused anymore. I had been galvanized into action.

I turned the pattern book over, leaving it open to mark the quilt block. "Tomorrow I'll pull out that fabric," I said through a yawn to Hobbes, and we returned to bed for a thankfully dreamless sleep.

FOUR

Seven Sisters

THE NEXT EVENING I MET the mysterious Wombats. They were gathered in a small alcove in the back of Ivy's Restaurant, a cafe on the opposite side of the park, just to the north of the eastern gate. The gate of the eagle and the morning sun, I thought as I passed under the stone archway. The east is where we look to the dawn, and illumination and birth, I reminded myself hopefully as I walked from the darkness of the park to the streetlit sidewalk outside.

I had crossed the park and eaten lunch at Ivy's several times but I'd never gone there after dark, and walking into the dimly lit restaurant felt like joining a meeting of Mafia Donnas. I half expected Momma Corleone to make me an offer I couldn't refuse. Two lumps, please. The whole place had a tight, nighttime closed-in feeling. There was a greasy steaminess in the long, thin room from the day of hot cooking in the kitchen. The lamps which hung over each table cast dim pools amongst the shadows and humps of empty furniture. The booths were vacant and even the counter where regulars had sat looked lonely for company. I was low with despair and worry as the full impact of the redevelopment proposal hit home like a wrecking ball. My position and my future were suddenly in jeopardy. I was in danger of losing my home and my livelihood at the same time. I had never felt so financially vulnerable, even after Jack died. The irony was that when I came to Clareville I thought I'd gotten rid of my "stuff." The reality was that I'd just exchanged it for another set of stuff. Stuff that I was afraid to lose, like Jo said.

I had lost my amused interest in this group of little old ladies and wondered why I was bothering to attend their meeting since

I was in no mood for socializing. I suppose I was anticipating something more than the half dozen women I found in the restaurant. I was used to much larger businesswomen's meetings and hadn't scaled down my expectations. Naturally, I had presumed gray hair. These were Wombats after all—women of menopause. Now I saw that these women looked like housewives or grannies, not like movers and shakers in town. Laurel and Hardy came to mind. "This is another fine mess you've gotten me into," I-Hardy, said silently to Jo-Laurel.

Jo read my disappointment and smiled. "You were expecting IBM executives, maybe?" she asked playfully. Her amusement suggested that she had experienced this response before. It's no wonder that small-towners take a long time to warm up to big-city newcomers. We arrive with stereotyped thinking written all over us. Appearances are often deceiving—not everyone in the city is intelligent and aware, and not everyone in the country is a rube. Often, people in the country just don't make a point of trying to prove how smart they are.

Ivy poured mugs of coffee for everyone and brief introductions took place before we got down to business, Terrorist business I hoped. I hadn't forgotten why I was there. Ever since the town Council meeting I was itching to *do* something but I had no idea what .

I had already met the owner of the restaurant, "Aunt Ivy." No relation to *Uncle* Al Brown. Ivy ran the only diner on the town square. She was another Wombat whose business and life were threatened by the redevelopment plan. Ivy was all of five feet tall and eighty pounds, a thin plain woman with a soft voice and remnant English accent. I learned that she had immigrated to America with her first husband who had a dream to open a restaurant. She looked as though she had worked and worried hard ever since, sweating over stoves from five in the morning until past eleven at night. I presumed that when her husband died, Ivy was left to run her cafe alone. I felt sorry for her. She was then caring for an invalid second husband twenty years older than her. What a terrible burden on those thin shoulders, I thought. Yet despite it all she sponsored girls' softball teams every Summer—called "Ivy's League." And that wasn't all.

She and "Aunt Millie," another of the women present, hosted a TV show called "As We See It" on the cable system, locally known as KORN-TV. They were the Siskel and Ebert of Clareville. They were the town conscience, the town voice, the town crankies. Any time I caught one of their twenty-minute programs, they were disagreeing about something. I wasn't sure what the programs were supposed to be about. One time they were cooking, and arguing about the best shortbread recipe. Another time they were sitting outside Johnson's Garden Center, arguing about fertilizer. The only common thread seemed to be their monumental disagreements. At some point in every show one of them would inevitably enlist the hapless cameraman to be their arbitrator, tell-all taste tester, or voice of the common man rebuttal witness. He would dutifully shuffle on-camera, taste, grunt and exit as soon as possible. I was in stitches the day they had him smelling fertilizer.

Where Aunt Ivy looked like your favorite aunt, a comfortable familiar sort of person, Aunt Millie looked as if the country club was her natural habitat but that she didn't take it the least bit seriously. Her accent was broad Bostonian and words with "ar" at the end became "ah." She was tall and slim, a well-but-discreetly dressed patrician-looking woman with dark hair and a distinctive gray streak at the temples. Her fine features reminded me of Anne Bancroft and I was immediately drawn to her. She was sophisticated, or maybe it was just the pearls she wore over her cashmere sweaterset. I always think pearls look so elegant and say "old money." Millie wore old pearls which her husband's "new money" had bought. I suspected it would be hard to get to know this woman, but I sensed it would be worth the effort. There was more to her than her cool and contained appearance revealed.

On TV, Aunt Ivy tended to be intensely serious, often appearing holding a sheaf of papers. She would research the topic at hand and quote statistics to support her position, appealing to the viewer's reason. Aunt Millie on the other hand had a sarcastic, rapier wit and tended to go for the common sense approach, appealing to the viewer's sense of humor and the absurd. Either one would have been a formidable politician, I thought.

Apparently, the only thing they ever agreed on was the town square. Keep it the way it is, they concurred. Which created another level of difficulty.

You see, "Aunt Millie," Millicent Brown was "Uncle Al" Brown's wife. Politics did make strange bedfellows indeed. Aunt Millie fell unequivocally on the side of preserving the town square, whereas Mayor Al stood equivocally on the side of preserving the peace, from a fence-sitting position. Now, I admire fair-handedness, but this matter had become life and death to me. There is a Greek legend about the women of Athens who went on strike and refused to make love until the men stopped making war. It was probably the origin of the Sixties hippie slogan "make love, not war,"and I secretly hoped that like the Greek women before her, Millie had adjourned Mayor Al's marital meetings, or connubial counselling, until he saw the light and squashed this stupid proposal. Strange bedfellows indeed.

Then there was Jo, of course, widow and retired business owner. It turned out she had never taught a quilting class before I "asked" her to. Apparently, lack of prior experience was never considered a handicap to her. "Until you ride a bicycle, you don't know how to ride a bicycle, do you?" she had told me, smiling and shrugging. Which was probably one of the best attitudes she could pass on to her students. I was growing terribly fond of her and her enigmatic philosophies.

Next was Ruth, who ran a hair salon on the square. Her figure resembled a round barrel on thin sticks topped by over-teased blond-gray hair. She was heavily made up and looked a little on the hard side, and I would have typecast her as a barmaid or truckstop waitress. Her raucous laughter underlined her devil-take-the-hindmost attitude. At first she seemed to have an easy, down-to-earth friendliness I liked and she kept reaching over to pat my arm whenever she made a point.

There was Marlene who barely qualified for the Wombat dis-
tinction, being in her early middle age. She had begged to join and
even offered to produce a doctor's certificate as proof of menopause! It's a mental age, she was told, not a physiological one.
Apparently, I too, qualified on merit, not hormones, since I run a
quilting shop and quilting is traditionally, and incorrectly, associated with little old ladies. Actually, I wasn't terribly sure why I had
been invited. So far it seemed to be an arbitrary selection process.

I learned that Marlene, who was a large woman with flawless
ebony skin, worked in real estate and interior decorating. I learned
much later that her soft Southern accent and good-natured humor belied her great fortitude and sacrifice. She specialized in old
properties and renovation but she was just as good at selling a
townhouse or suburban semi. She wore tight blue jeans and a
bright orange tie-dyed t-shirt. I didn't think they made tie-dyed
shirts anymore. Then I realized it was probably an *original* Sixties
t-shirt, and *that* was impressive dressing-down. Anyone who kept
old clothes like that would be a great quilter, I thought.

Marlene's real estate office was managed by Little Al and she
had been the early-warning Cassandra to alert the Wombats about
the redevelopment plan as she kept her ear to the ground for us, I
mean them. Was I already considering myself one of the Wombats?

The last and oldest member of these civil anarchists was Viola,
who was eighty-four. She was slightly deaf but spry and lively, and
she had a ready laugh, even though she walked painfully with a
cane. "Broken hip, you know. Doc says if I break the other one,
they're going to have to shoot me!" she quipped. "Or was it the
vet who said that?"

Viola had been a history teacher. Years ago, she had even taught
Jo. When they told her she was too old to teach, she became the
town librarian, a post she held for twenty years after her so-called
retirement. She didn't say much during the meeting but her little
bird-like head bobbed back and forth with the conversation, and
she paid close attention to everything that was said. I'm not sure
why Viola belonged to the Wombats; she had never been a busi-

nesswoman per se. But when you're eighty-four I guess you can belong to any club you want to join. And then again, perhaps she had been a terrorist in her day. I thought, *that's* what I want to be like when I'm in my eighties. As with Grama, Viola had survived for many decades, and her mere existence and membership gave the Wombats a broader perspective on history and society. After all, she had lived through the world wars, the invention of cars, telephones, airplanes, television, computers, refrigerators and just about everything else that we take for granted today. She could actually remember days in her life before such inventions. It made you stop and think. I hope to acquire that there-was-a-time-before perspective when I'm older. Come to think of it maybe I already have it. I can remember life before computers. Oh dear, I am older than I thought.

Grama should be here, I sighed. Jo was right, she would have fit right in with these women.

My thoughts were interrupted by Jo saying, "We all know why we're here tonight. So let's get down to it. This redevelopment proposal has now officially gone to council, and it has to be stopped! What are we going to do about it?"

"We could start a formal petition," offered Ivy immediately. Apparently she had come with the idea already in mind.

"We could chain ourselves to the trees in the park!" Marlene laughed.

"They'd just chop us down with the trees," replied Millie.

"We could kidnap Al Junior and ship him out of town in a box with no air holes," Ruth offered. "Sorry, Mil," she apologized, having momentarily forgotten that Millie was Al Junior's mother. Ah, another complication, I realized.

Millie laughed. "That's okay. There have been times when I considered doing that myself!"

"Al is only doing what he thinks is right. It's just not what *we* think is right. We have to convince him, and the rest, otherwise," Jo rejoined.

"What does Big Al think?" We all turned to look at Aunt Millie.

"Well . . . he wants to consider all the sides," she began slowly. She took a long drink of coffee.

"As usual," snorted Ivy. Millie gave her a withering look as she carefully replaced her mug on the table.

"Can't you get him to do something?" Marlene asked.

"Never been able to in the past. He hasn't said what he thinks. I don't think he'll try to convince anyone in either direction. It's pretty hard for him to go against his own son, if that is what he wants to do. They have a hard enough time getting along these days," Millie said sadly.

"That must be tough on you," Marlene commiserated. "I have two teenage boys, fourteen and thirteen," she explained, turning to me, "and I know what it feels like to be pushed and pulled between them and their father."

"The worst thing is you just get your kids through teen-age and then you hit menopause!" Ruth joked.

"I thought menopause was the *reward* for enduring teenagers!" Marlene exclaimed with a hearty laugh.

"It's a wonder anyone survives parenthood," Jo commented.

"Well, it's not so bad," Millie responded. "Al is a wonderful father. And Little Al is a wonderful son. I love them both. They just seem to be at odds these days. Maybe because I'm pushing Big Al too much. I'm sure they must discuss the redevelopment project when they are alone together but since I feel so strongly about this proposal, maybe Al thinks he has to take my side and that puts him against his son." She obviously felt some guilt about their strained relationship. "I guess only time will tell," she sighed heavily and poured herself a second mug of coffee.

"What about the rest of Council?" asked Ruth, tactfully changing the subject.

"I'm sure Frank Dempsey is for this proposal," Jo answered. "He'll be a pain in the butt. Remember the ruckus he caused over the traffic lights."

"What does he care? He already moved his hardware store out to the highway," replied Ivy. I had noticed the abandoned, boarded-up store front down the street from my place. At least he hadn't sold out to Little Al Junior yet. Perhaps he was hoping the land prices would go up and he could cash in at that time.

"But he still owns the property on the square and stands to make a bundle either way," Marlene said.

I raised my hand to speak and waited my turn.

"He's probably happy to see the old town center die so that people will be forced out to his store on the highway," Ivy argued.

I was trying to follow all the lines of thought about people I mostly didn't know as the women discussed each of the Councillors in turn. My hand was still raised and after a while I began to feel foolishly polite. I felt like the kid in school who had to leave the room, patiently waiting, finally having to prop up one arm with the other.

Eventually everyone looked at me and fell silent.

"I think that Ivy's petition is a good idea," I offered. "I don't know much about politics but it seems that if the public supports keeping the old square, then Council will vote that way."

"That's pretty naive but I guess it wouldn't hurt," Millie commented.

"I thought that was *democracy*," Ivy said softly.

"I've also been thinking about Al Junior's proposal and it seems to have a lot of merit," I continued.

"What! Whose side are you on!" Marlene exclaimed, hurling herself forward in her chair.

"Wait. Let her finish," Jo scolded with a restraining hand on Marlene's arm.

"If parking is a problem, then people won't come downtown. That's bad for business. When I first moved here I couldn't even get parked near my own shop. Even with a petition—and I'm not sure why anyone would sign it—I'm not sure we can defeat the proposal simply because we *don't like it*. It seems we have to come up with another plan that has *more* appeal," I said.

"Like what?" Ivy asked.

"I don't know yet. But I think it's easier to get people to agree to something they like than to get them to take a stand against something they don't like," I reasoned.

"You're right. That's people," Marlene shrugged agreement and relaxed back into her chair.

"Makes sense," Ivy agreed.

"There must be *another* way of looking at this," I carried on. "Instead of tearing everything down. There must be a more creative, constructive thing we can do."

"Well, all the years I've been on Main Street, I've always complained about the parking myself," said Ruth. "I often have customers parking blocks away. I don't like losing the park, but I'm losing business because of the limited parallel parking along the shop fronts." She paused. Then she appeared to think twice about continuing and waved us off that she was finished. I wondered what her unspoken thought had been.

Ivy had been lining up coffee spoons on the table in front of her. "What if it was angle parking instead," she suggested, turning the spoons at a 45-degree angle in demonstration. "You can get more cars in that way."

"There isn't enough room. The streets are too narrow," Millie objected.

We all sat looking at the spoons.

"Not if you use only this outside lane for traffic and have one-way traffic around the park," Ivy continued.

It hit us all.

"That's brilliant! Why not!" Marlene exclaimed.

"There's an alternative plan for you," I pointed out.

"Surely Al Junior or someone on Council must have thought of this before," Ruth countered.

"Not if you have a vested interest," I replied. "Sometimes people don't want to see alternatives once they've convinced themselves that there is only one way to look at a situation. Al Junior's proposal answers the problem in a way that benefits him. We need alternatives, like this idea, which suit us. How many more spaces would that provide?" I asked Ivy.

"I don't know but I could get a survey tape tomorrow and figure it out properly," she offered.

"That's great! That's exactly what we need," I encouraged.

"That's really good, Ivy," Millie complimented her nemesis.

"We could draw out a proper plan. I could do it on my computer if you like," she offered helpfully.

"Thanks. Okay," Ivy agreed. Apparently there were times when they could work cooperatively together. "At a guess, we could probably double the parking spaces. But it's not enough, is it, love?" She looked at me.

I shook my head no.

"Well, Al Junior wants to tear down the whole block opposite the town hall. Those postwar buildings are ugly. No one would miss them. Why not get him to build a parking lot there? And he'd be welcome to the parking lot revenue," Marlene suggested.

We all nodded except Ruth. "Small compensation for the loss of major redevelopment money," she commented sarcastically.

"But not the Armbruster building," Viola finally spoke. She had been listening all the while to our back and forth talk, her gray head bobbing like a spectator at a tennis match.

"The what?" I asked, turning my attention to her.

"The stone building on the corner," she explained. "It was General Armbruster's headquarters during the Civil War. Before that it was a famous traveler's inn and tavern built by the British on the old coach road. It was called The Hay Wain back then," she explained.

I had wondered why someone hadn't done something to fix up that terrific old three-storey building. There were high weeds growing around it through cracks in the neglected sidewalk. Scraggly vines clung despairingly to the weatherbeaten edifice and the deep casement windows on the ground floor were boarded up with a rag-tag assortment of lumber to keep vandals out. The wide green door and shutters hadn't seen fresh paint in decades. It was hard to imagine it had been an important and bustling commercial center in days gone by.

"Imagine that!" Ruth said with sudden animation. "I didn't know that."

"There's lots of history in this town most people don't know about," Viola continued. "He shouldn't be allowed to tear down a nice old building like that. It ought to be against the law!" she declared defiantly.

"But it *is* against the law!" Marlene exclaimed. She slapped her forehead. "I'm so stupid! I should have known better. If it's a historic site, we can get a 'Preservation Order' to stop him from tearing it down," she explained.

"But wouldn't we have to have documents and proof that it was worth preserving?" Ivy asked.

"Hmm. You're right," Marlene agreed.

"Shoot. There's all kinds of stuff like that," Viola dismissed the objection with a wave of her hand. Her body was bird-like but her voice was surprisingly strong.

"Where?" I asked.

"In the library basement. Nobody's ever been interested in looking at those musty old documents. I catalogued them a hundred years ago and stored them away."

"Do you think they're still there?" I asked. "Can we get access to them?"

"If we can, then I can get a Preservation Order," Marlene said. "We have to act fast though. If Al Junior starts to tear the building down anyway, there's nothing we can do. He owns it. He can easily get a Demolition Order from the Town Clerk." She turned to Millie. "Any idea what he's up to?"

"Since he knows I disapprove of the idea, he doesn't talk to me anymore. He used to when he was buying up the properties on the square. He always said he would tear it down. It needs too much repair. I had no idea he was going to tear everything down—" Millie trailed off unhappily. Despite the obvious boarding school bearing that trained her to sit upright and properly poised, there was a definite depressed slope to her shoulders.

I felt sorry for Millie. She seemed to be on the defensive, on account of her son. She wasn't responsible for the actions of the men in her life. Yet like all women, she felt the need to fix and heal, to build bridges of understanding.

"Well, that's a good start. At least we can try to stop that. I know sometimes in the city, not acquiring or being able to use one key site will stop a redevelopment project," I said, trying to sound convincing.

"Really?" they all echoed in surprise.

"Sure." I hoped I sounded encouraging. "Sure. It could work. I was at a conference in Toronto one time and downtown they have a huge modern shopping mall that was built right around an old church and a couple of historic buildings because they couldn't buy the property and demolish them. It was an odd construction I guess, but it actually looked very interesting when it was finished. It could work," I repeated.

"That would fix Little Al's wagon!" Jo nodded. Everyone was pleased.

"But what about the buildings on the other side? Al owns half of them, too. And what about the problem of attracting more people downtown? It's fine to park but you have to have a reason to come here," Ruth pointed out.

"Well, the merchants who are there now could do more to help themselves—ourselves," Ivy insisted. "Some of the Main Street merchants, of course not you, love," she said to me, "are really behind the times. They need to update what they're doing."

"That's true," Ruth finally agreed to something. "If I still cut hair like I did twenty years ago, I wouldn't have any customers either. Sometimes it's embarrassing to be on the same block as those stores. I probably shouldn't say this, but I've had to give some serious thought to selling my place to Little Al. And sometimes I'm tempted."

So that was her unvoiced comment.

"You wouldn't!" Ivy exclaimed indignantly. Everyone else's face showed the same shocked reaction.

Ruth just shrugged. "Why do people go to the big fancy malls? Easy parking, good service, selection and good prices."

"So how do we change that?" I asked.

"We can't. It's too big a project," Ruth answered. It irritated me that she found the negative in everything. We had enough problems without that.

Ignoring the pessimism, Millie said, "Well, the whole place could start with a facelift. Most of the shop fronts look dowdy and uninviting."

We all nodded agreement.

"But it takes money and a coordinated plan to improve things. How do we get everyone to cooperate?" I prompted.

"You could form a Downtown Merchant's Association," suggested Jo. "Talk to everyone in a group. Convince them to act cohesively. In their own best interests. There's always more power in operating as an organized group."

"Maybe as a group the merchants would qualify for some financial assistance in renovating," Marlene suggested. "We could talk to the bank."

"Sounds like the bank is already in bed with the developers." I told them about my letter from the bank manager.

"Well, they're not the only bank," Marlene insisted. "I know from putting together a lot of real estate deals, sometimes you have to shop it around. For instance, I heard of one small town brewer with a one hundred year old family business who was looking for some expansion money. He ended up going to *eighty-eight* banks before he secured the funding for his business!"

"Whew!" We all exclaimed. Now that's perseverance, I thought.

"And you can bet if another bank is interested, the local bank will want back into the picture, so they don't lose the business. They'll go wherever they can make money. That's their business," Marlene concluded.

"Well that would improve the shopping, but it still doesn't justify keeping the park itself. If people don't use it, it might as well be a parking lot!" Ruth proclaimed stubbornly.

"That's true." We nodded morosely.

"You know. I have to admit I've always eyed the park land

myself and wished I could open a little outdoor cafe in the park . . ."

We all turned to look at Ivy.

"It could be so pleasant sitting in the park, having high tea, scones and strawberry jam, and whipped cream cakes. . . ." She pantomined delicately picking up a teacup with pinkie finger extended.

We sat looking at her in surprise.

"What?" she said when she saw our stares. "What did I say?"

"Why not?" I asked.

"Yeah. Why not have a cafe in the park? That sort of thing could start drawing people downtown, and encourage them to use the park more," Marlene pointed out.

"But how do we do that?" I asked.

"Pretty easy," Jo explained. "You just get Council to vote on a 'Temporary Use Permit'. Temporary, like April to October and away you go. You couldn't put anything permanent in the park but if you located your cafe directly across from the restaurant, Ivy, you could service it from there."

"Could you handle all that extra work?" I asked Ivy.

"You mean all that extra business!" she exclaimed with a laugh. "What do you think! I'd just offer a limited menu of sandwiches and brunch and tea-time sorts of things, and hire some extra waitresses. I have a couple of girls who would like more hours but I can't afford to give it to them now."

"That's another great idea. Every one should be part of our counter-proposal," I said. Ivy had obviously had more than a couple of idle daydreams about her cafe idea. I wondered why she hadn't tried it out. Maybe she never told her dream to anyone before, so no one was able to help her with it. If you have an idea you have to put it out there to the universe to make it happen, I reflected.

"You know, if business was really good, I'd hire a real cook and get out of the kitchen more myself—" She said as she continued her pleasant reverie.

There were big dreams inside this little woman. Why shouldn't they come true, I wondered. I wasn't the only one whose goals and aspirations were centered around the town square. Its greenery had inspired other healthy and growing visions.

"That sort of thing draws tourists as well," Jo pointed out. "Especially if we have a historic building to show off."

"And what about concerts in the bandstand?" I suggested. Every morning I looked out on the forlorn little wooden gazebo and wondered when the town had last gone there to hear joyful music.

"Where would we get a *band?*" Ruth asked in a nasal whine that in spite of myself I was beginning to dislike. Her objections were automatic, I decided. She was just one of those people who always sees the waterglass as half-empty instead of half-full. She probably didn't even realize she was doing it.

"I don't know," I answered. "Maybe it's just piped-in music to start with but we could come up with events like festivals, or flea markets, or antique shows, which draw people to the park. At Christmas there could be carols and a lighted tree. Then people would have a reason to want to keep it. Maybe then they'd sign a petition."

"Right," everyone nodded. Surprisingly, even Ruth who had been our Devil's Advocate finally had to agree.

"So why can't *we* make a counter-proposal to Council," I suggested. No one seemed to have a reason not to.

"Okay. What do we have to do?" Millie asked.

"Well, we've already come up with some good ideas. Ivy, you figure out how much more parking we could create using angle parking and a lot on Al Junior's land. Millie can draw a plan of it on her computer. Ruth, why don't you, Ivy and I organize a merchants' meeting since we're the ones directly affected by the redevelopment proposal? And Marlene and Viola need to obtain the historic documents from the library and start working on a Preservation Order. We need to act fast before Al Junior gets wind of anything," I summarized.

"We'll go first thing in the morning," they nodded.

"Little Al was well prepared at the meeting. We have to be, too. We need facts, and figures, and documentation. This has to look serious and professional, and most of all possible, for people to back it," I asserted.

"I'll write up the petition," Jo offered, "and print some copies and get clipboards. What about some flyers? I can have them printed at the office."

"I can talk to an architect friend of mine about how much it would cost to renovate the other shops on Main and Elm Streets. Then we'll know what to present to the bank," Marlene said.

"Excellent," Jo complimented her.

"I'd like to see them all put back into their original style, with proper Olde Worlde signs to be consistent with the historic Armbruster building," said Viola. "It could be a real tourist attraction." We nodded again.

Millie spoke up then. "Al might not openly support or oppose this proposal but I'll have him give me some names of people who might be interested in financing the renovation. I'll talk to them myself. If we can put together a consortium of private investors, we may not need the banks."

"Great idea," I encouraged her. "That way the merchants could pay back the improvement loan at good terms over a long time."

"Must be nice to have friends in high places," Jo teased.

"I can tell you, it wouldn't cost much to put a cafe in the park. All I need are some weatherproof tables and chairs and umbrellas," said Ivy. "I think I can find someone who'd donate them. I'd be willing to pay for the rest myself." She was even ready to invest in her dream. I liked this woman more and more.

"You know Sousa's band came here to play once," Viola reminisced. Viola was our link with the past, our own golden oldie.

"The bandshell is a wreck," Ruth pointed out.

"Oh, what does a bit of paint cost!" I countered irritably.

"Too much if you don't have it," Ruth snapped. "Who's going to pay for it? And what about the footpaths. Some of them are downright treacherous. They need replacing."

I blew out a puff of breath in exasperation.

Viola had gone adrift for a few moments and was apparently

stuck on the enchanting image of a marching band in the park.
"You could hire music students during the Summer," she suggested, coming up with a band for the concerts.

"There you go! A band!" I exclaimed and nudged Ruth's shoulder to make sure she didn't miss the point.

Marelene had been quiet for several minutes. She finally spoke.
"You know, I took my kids to Disneyworld once and they have this
roadway . . . It's made of bricks, and people *buy* the bricks. Their
name is put on it and then the bricks are built into the road—"

"So?" Ruth said.

"So, why couldn't we do that? Sell bricks to fund rebuilding
the footpaths and then incorporate the bricks into the paths,"
Marlene suggested.

"And maybe we could bury Ruth. She's a brick," Millie said
under her breath but loud enough for us all to hear anyway. Ruth
glared at her.

"I'm just being realistic," Ruth pointed out defensively.

"Since when is your so-called reality-check an excuse for saying 'no' to everything in life?"

"This is great," I jumped in. It looked as if a real fight was
brewing. "I love the idea of selling bricks. It could get people
involved with the park again. Families would bring their kids to
see their piece of the park. These are all terrific ideas." I was
excited by the prospect. "We can make this happen! At least we
can give it a darn good try."

I started to believe it myself. Funny that. Sometimes when
you set out to encourage and convince others, I reflected, you
end up encouraging and convincing yourself. I knew that whenever I decided to engage the world I inevitably had an impact on
other people's lives, just as others had on mine. We're all connected. There is a time to quilt alone and there is a time to quilt
together. The quilt I make from my solitude reaches out to touch
the lives of others with its beauty and artistry, but the quilt we
make together captures everyone's heart and binds us in community, and love. Like scrap pieces of fabric this disparate group of

women had been brought together, I thought, chosen by the creator's hand, and stitched into a complete design with purpose and perfect placement. The Wombats, thank heavens, were going to be my partners in adversity. I wasn't alone in this trouble after all. Sometimes when troubles fall on us, I remembered, we don't realize that there are hidden hands already in motion coming to help us. That there are allies and resources we can tap into by simply setting out with intention and determination.

It looked as though there was going to be a lot to do over the summer months. But at least, together, the Wombats had a battle plan. We all hugged in a very un-military manner before we said goodnight.

On the way home, I thought of an old joke.

A river has flooded its banks and all the nearby houses are slowly being engulfed by water. The residents evacuate. All except one man who says, "God will save me." A neighbor in a rowboat comes by and offers to carry him to safety, but he refuses saying, "God will save me." The flood waters flow higher and he is forced upstairs to the second story of his home. Then the Coast Guard comes by and offers to take him to safety, but he refuses saying, "God will save me." As the flood rises higher he is finally forced to the roof. Finally a helicopter flies by and the rescuers offer to take him to safety. Yet again he refuses, saying, "God will save me." In the end the foolish man drowns and goes up to the Pearly Gates. When he meets his Maker he angrily demands, "Why did you let me drown? I believed in you! Why didn't you save me?" and God's answer was, "Who do you think sent the rowboat, the Coast Guard and the helicopter!"

We don't always recognize the resources that we have.

The Wombats had already been in existence before I arrived in town. Although they didn't know it themselves, it was as if they had been waiting there to come to my assistance. Assistance that I didn't know I needed or could use until now. To receive tea, I reminded myself, hold an empty cup. I had to be open to those positive forces. If I fell into despair or fear, or denial, I would not recognize the help when it came.

Maybe the Wombats were only a leaky rowboat, but it was rescue.

And then again, when I looked back on my own life, perhaps there were times when I had been the rowboat for others.

I LEFT THE WOMBATS MEETING feeling light-hearted and confident but by the time I returned alone to the little shop on Main Street and fought with the lock and chain, the old doubts started to creep back. That stupid chain had begun to weigh as heavily on me as the chains on Joseph Marley's ghost. I felt a cold darkness in my soul. What could a small group of middle-aged women accomplish? We had no power, no money. We were just whistling into the wind. There were power and money and the blue suits of big business in this thing against us. Who were we to try and stop this, I thought mournfully. And me—I'm no David against this Goliath. I'm just a middle-aged widow who tried to dabble in business without knowing what she was getting herself into. My little troubles didn't matter.

And yet, there is a higher cause.

I patted Hobbes, put on the kettle and sat in the bay window overlooking the park. On the one hand while I ruminated on my sense of futility, my other clinical and watchful self had an inspiration. I reminded myself that in psychology there is a term called "delusions of grandeur" and it's considered a mental illness by western medical standards. It's ironic, I realized, but there is no equivalent term for the opposite condition, for the delusion that we don't matter, that we are too insignificant to make a difference. Yet we all suffer from it. Why don't we start that recycling program in our neighborhood? Because we think there is nothing we can do as one little individual. Why don't we pick up that one discarded tin can? Call that charity and offer help? Write that protest letter to a senator or congressman? Because we believe that our small actions have no importance. But small does not necessarily mean insignificant. The reality is that it's only through the everyday actions of every little individual, united and multiplied, that anything great ever happens.

Perhaps we should call the condition "delusions of insignificance" and then it could be officially considered an illness, a spiritual illness. We would then be taking steps to cure it by teaching people that everyone matters, that everyone can make a difference, that to think otherwise is the delusion.

And yet, even with that realization, I was imbedded in feelings of futility and it was hard to pick myself up. When would I learn that getting unstuck doesn't necessarily mean coming unglued? The greater the trouble, the greater the need for support. It was one of those things that would take sympathetic bolstering and encouragement from others. It would take another hidden hand coming into play.

The phone rang. It was Jennifer.

"I've been calling all evening. Are you alright?" she asked in concern.

Isn't it remarkable how people can be so invisibly tuned into each other? For no apparent reason we're impelled to call or write to someone just at the time when they need to hear from us. Or else we ourselves receive the call we need. What is this fragile thread that connects us? Something as lofty and directed as the hand of God? Or is the heart such a delicate biological organ that it can distinguish the distant cries of the beloved as a whale can hear its mate's song across hundreds of miles of ocean?

"Oh yes. I'm fine. I do go out, you know," I chided her affectionately. "I went to meet the Wombats."

"The who? Mom, are you alright?" she repeated with a laugh.

"Yes." I laughed too at how silly it sounded. "The Wombats are part of the local women's business association. They call themselves Women of Menopause Business Association and Terroritst Society." I explained the acronym and Jennifer laughed again.

"That sounds great," she sighed heavily. I was so caught up in remembrances of the evening that at first I missed the doleful undertone to her voice.

"They're really terrific women," I said.

"Mom, remember that first night when Jo came into the shop? She said, 'everything that you seek, is seeking you.' That sounded a lot like Grama. Is it true? Are you getting everything you seek?"

"Well, I don't know about getting everything I seek, but in a perverse sort of way, yes, I suppose things are seeking me out, though I don't know why sometimes," I answered.

"How do you mean?"

"Well, I always try to seek out the positive things in life but sometimes a negative thing happens instead. In that case I try to look on it as something I must have needed to have happen, to learn a lesson. I know that it's one of the dualities of life that without sometimes experiencing what is hard and necessary I can't ultimately succeed. In other words, sometimes there is joy and then pain. And other times there is pain and then joy." I also wanted to tell her that it's an essential responsibility of growing into mature womanhood to embrace both contradictions. To deny either was to deny the force of life that flows through us as women. Without pain there is no birth; without birth there is no pain.

"Does that help you get through the agonies?" she asked. It was her second pointed question and I wondered what was happening in her life to create the sudden philosophical curiosity. Jennifer is not normally given to much introspection.

"Honey, I wish I could say it did. The truth is, sometimes I still get stuck on one side of the teeter-totter or the other." I told her about the town meeting, the Wombats' battleplan and my rollercoaster feelings. She was immediately concerned for my welfare and somehow I don't think she was impressed with our chances for success. "I guess I'm not a very good psychologist, am I?"

"But that just makes you human," she countered sympatheticly, "and a great Mom."

"Thanks for the reassurance."

It's so nice, I realized, to have grown daughters to talk to as friends and equals, and no longer like children I have to explain everything to, or be strong for.

"So, what's up with you?" I asked, and she began to talk about the troubles she was having with her boyfriend.

Jennifer had been dating Jim for two years and she claimed she was happy with him. He certainly treated her well. He was always doing nice little things to please her. He was a pretty romantic guy and she admitted that he would be "a good catch." Fish or flounder, I wondered.

"So what's the problem?"

"Oh Mom, I don't know. It's just that sometimes I feel so . . . stifled!" she moaned. Jennifer tends to the melodramatic at the best of times.

"What do you mean?" I prompted.

"You know we have a lot of great times together." She paused and breathed heavily. "We go to terrific places and we sure laugh a lot."

"Yes. So?"

"And I feel so guilty about complaining—"

"Yes. So?"

"I guess that's the problem. Every weekend he wants us to do absolutely everything together. I never seem to have any time alone. I can't see my friends without him coming along. Unfortunately, all my friends think he's a great guy. It's worse than having Suzie tag along after me when we were kids. He never goes out by himself with his friends either. I feel like he's hung around my neck all the time. He wants me to share every one of his interests and he wants to be involved in all of my interests. It's like we're joined at the hip!"

I could imagine her gesturing wildly as her anger tumbled out over the telephone. Jennifer has always been independent and I could understand how it would be a burden to her. She needs air, and space. She needs an inter-dependent relationship where both parties give and take, come and go, orbiting around each other in love, not desperately clinging for mutual survival. At first she had been flattered by his overwhelming attentiveness, but now . . .

"Couples are supposed to share interests," I pointed out.

"Yeah, I know." Now she sounded depressed.

"Have you told him how you feel?"

"Yeah. And he says if I love him I wouldn't want to spend time alone or with anyone else."

Oh, oh, I thought. "If you love me . . ." Four of the most manipulative and destructive words in any relationship. I hate to hear young people beat each other up with that controlling exploitation. I wanted to say, "If you love him you owe him the truth."

"Why do you think he's like that?" I asked.

She thought for a moment. "I guess he's insecure."

I nodded "uh-huh" into the phone.

"But Mom, I love him and I tell him so all the time. He's such a great guy in every other respect. Why is he so insecure?"

"You may never know, honey. Perhaps his family background—"

"And that's another thing," she interrupted. "He always wants us to spend time with his family. They're nice enough people but he can't seem to do anything without involving them in what we do. It's like they're co-dependent or something. I guess he's as clingy to his parents as he is to me. Come to think of it, maybe his whole family is like that." She paused to breathe and think, and the pendulum swung the other way. "I shouldn't complain really. They treat me well." Another pause. It was like listening to a ping-pong ball as she waffled back and forth between her anger and her guilt. "He wants to get married . . ."

That was something of a surprise but not really unexpected. "Honey, that would be wonderful news, but you don't sound very pleased so I won't congratulate you yet. You're obviously having your doubts. You need to be sure marriage is the right thing for you, and for Jim too. If it doesn't work for you, then ultimately it won't work for him either."

"But it would kill Jim if I broke up with him. I don't want to hurt him," she cried.

Oh boy, I thought. Not that too. If you leave me I'll kill myself. Run, Jen, run, I wanted to yell.

How often we cause suffering for ourselves in our vain attempts to care for others. She would rather hold back her truth and her integrity out of "love" for Jim than treat him like an adult who is capable of handling his own destiny. I resisted telling her that we have no right to make those decisions for other people, to force our own agenda for pity and compassion on someone else as if we are the all-knowing parent and they the dis-abled child. Most of us can barely handle our own struggles effectively, much less those of others.

"If it doesn't work for you, it won't work for him either," I repeated.

Jennifer's silence indicated her concession to the point. I suspected she already knew what I was saying but needed to hear it out loud.

"But I don't want to break up with him," she groaned. "After all I've got two years invested in this relationship. I don't want to start all over again. I just want him to stand on his own two feet and to give me some space."

All I could say was, "Jen, you know you can't go into a marriage hoping that someone will change. Remember, what you see is what you get. Marriage by itself will end up changing both of you in ways you can't even conceive of yet. Don't go into it with expectations to change someone—and the same advice applies to Jim. If he's expecting to change you, then he is wrong to go into it. As you say, you have two years invested already. Are you prepared to invest the rest of your life?" Jennifer was struggling with an age old dilemma. Young men go into marriage thinking nothing will change, that everything will be roses and candlelight forever, and young women think they will change everything. The men find out that everything changes and the women find out that nothing changes.

"Think of it this way, Honey," I said. "Statistically, you will probably live another fifty years and could be married for that long. That means you would spend another twenty-eight hundred weekends with Jim. Are you sure that's what you want?"

"Twenty-eight *hundred?*" she asked in surprise.

"Uh huh."

There was a long, long pause. "That's a good question, Mom," Jennifer sighed. "I really don't know. I guess I'd better find out."

Sometimes talking doesn't solve problems, but just hearing a caring sympathetic voice can ease the pain until a solution is found. There are so many chains on our hearts, I sighed to myself as I hung up the telephone. I had tried over the years since Jack died to teach my children to follow their hearts and integrity into love. How could I teach Jennifer that perhaps she now had to follow her heart *out* of love? Holding onto a dead love is a chain that holds you back from fully engaging the world. I meant to say, holding onto the wrong love . . .

I cupped my hand around Jack's locket.

Was I talking to myself?

IT WAS AFTER MIDNIGHT when we finally rang off, but there was something I had to do. I went downstairs to the dark shop. There was enough dim light from streetlights shining through the blinds for me to see my way around without bumping into anything until I flicked on the cutting table light. The first thing I did was take out a six-point star template from the rack and then started pulling "fat eighths" from the fabric bins. Fat eighths are simply generous eighth-of-a-yard cuts of fabric. They, along with "fat quarters", are popular with quilters because they're an easy way to buy small pre-cut amounts of many different fabrics which add color and variety to a quilt, without costing much money. Economy is still a quilting virtue, held over from the pioneer days of scarcity and frugality. It fits well into today's recycling efforts. I sat on my usual barstool and began cutting. I found that I enjoyed these quiet times, alone with my thoughts, in what had become my sacred time and space. The darkness around the table blanked out all the distractions and cares of the outside world. It helped me focus on the slow meditative work at hand, and released my creative feelings.

My fourth block is a *Seven Sisters* block. It's another traditional design comprised of a central six-point star surrounded on each point by six other six-point stars. However, instead of using the usual white or light colored background, I decided to use black. Black like the night sky and the gloom of despair against which my Seven Sisters stand out like the stars in the Pleiades constellation, shining stars to light the darkness with hope. Stars are an ancient symbol of celestial guidance or divine presence but they still need interpreting. We can follow a star to our destiny but only our experience as we travel and when we arrive will teach us anything. A star points the way—it's up to us to make the point.

In my *Seven Sisters* block, I'm the white star in the center. I used new fabric for this pattern because this block is for Jo and the Wombats, my new-found allies, my helpmates. We are the Seven Sisters, soul sisters. Each of the six surrounding stars that represented my six new friends and supporters form a rainbow of color. Violet, blue, green, yellow, orange, red. All the colors of the rainbow combine to form pure white light, complete light. Just as I gain completeness from the colors each of my sisters adds to me.

Winning or losing the impending battle to save my shop and the old town center didn't matter, I realized. I had already won because I'd found comrades in life. The connection to people was what mattered. It was the togetherness that counted. There is power in the group, and it gives power to the Self. That's the second delusion—that we are alone, unconnected to the whole.

"You have to find the ones you belong to," Jo had said the other night on the way home. "There's a circle of people you have to meet in life, are destined to meet. It's your life's work to find those people, complete the circle and fulfill your destiny. When you do, then you can die in peace."

I understood then what she had meant when she said, "All roads lead to home, spiritual home." It was the inner home, the home of the heart that we all seek. Sometimes finding these people was like searching through a maze. In the darkness, my life looked like a labyrinth. In the light, I found the thread to guide me out.

The Wombats were part of my spiritual family, and I'd come home.

FIVE

Monkey Wrench

I WAS STILL THINKING ABOUT HOME the next morning. From the windowseat, I looked around my apartment, thought about the shop below and gazed out at the park, struck by the abundance that surrounded me. I felt reassurance in the circle of women around me. As I sipped my coffee, I ruminated on a quote from James Michener—"This is the journey that men and women make, to find themselves. If they fail in this, it doesn't matter what else they find." I was so lost in philosophical thoughts, that it took me a few minutes to notice a white pickup truck parked outside, a few doors down the block. It had the emblem of the Fire Department on its side door. Hmmm, I smiled to myself, I wonder if my fireman's "mother" needs some more fabric.

A few minutes later, at opening time, I went downstairs. There is a back staircase which leads directly up to my apartment but the front door lock and chain can only be opened from the outside so twice a day I have to make the trip on the outside staircase to and from the shop. I fiddled with the annoying lock and chain on the door. I've got to get this fixed, I swore to myself for the upteenth time. As soon as I opened the shop and turned on the lights, sure enough there he was at my elbow. He must have stepped out of his truck as soon as he saw me at the door. My heart jumped a little.

"Good morning," I smiled as he crossed the threshold into the shop behind me. Hobbes had beat me into the shop via the inner staircase and sat waiting as I opened the door. It was a game we played every morning. I would say goodbye to Hobbes as I went out the door upstairs and he would tear downstairs to greet me

82

hello as I entered the shop below. I think he thought it was amusing.

"I remember you from last week. How's your mother's quilting?" I asked as I continued with my morning set-up routine, rolling up the blinds, turning on the lights and changing the "Closed" sign to "Come on in".

"Mother? Oh, fine, fine," he said in a voice that I thought was a few notes higher than I remembered. He cleared his throat and it returned to normal. "By the way, my name's Daniel. Daniel Fairbanks. And yours?" He followed me to the cash desk and extended his hand. Hobbes followed too and jumped up but kept his distance.

"Aggie," I replied as we shook hands briefly. His hand was warm and firm. "Angela, but everyone calls me Aggie."

"Texas A and M?" he asked.

When our hands separated he left his extended in midair near Hobbes and made a low crooning noise. This time Hobbes didn't retreat and after a couple of seconds Daniel stuck out his index finger, slowly reached over to Hobbes and rubbed it along his whiskers. "Hi buddy," he crooned as Hobbes reluctantly leaned into the caress in spite of himself. "No spitting today, buddy, okay?" he said softly. Daniel looked at me again with raised eyebrows, his question still hanging unanswered.

"Oh. Yes, A and M," I confirmed. Why was I so pleased that he recognized the moniker? "I met my husband there. He started everyone calling me Aggie," I explained. We had attended the Texas Agriculture and Mining University. The football team is affectionately known as the "Aggies".

"Does your husband still follow college ball?" he asked innocently, dropping his eyes again to Hobbes who was now purring enthusiastically at Daniel's touch. . . . Oh, what does he know, he's just a cat.

I suddenly realized that perhaps he too had checked out my hand for a wedding ring and hadn't found one. "Wish he did," I replied ruefully and then explained. "He died ten years ago." I automatically put my hand to the locket around my neck and held onto it.

"Sorry," he said gravely.

I waved him off with a shake of my head. "What can I do for you today?"

"I need blades for my rotary cutter. Uh, for mother's cutter," he stammered.

"For an elderly lady who doesn't get out much, your mother sure keeps up on all the latest techniques," I teased him lightly as I motioned us toward the notions rack where the packages of blades were hanging. "Perhaps if she can get out at all she would like to take one of our classes," I suggested.

"Oh, that wouldn't be possible," he protested and quickly turned his attention to the rack. He leaned forward, humming and intently reading the labels for an unnaturally long time before he reached out and selected a package of blades and handed them to me.

"That everything?" I asked. He nodded yes. "Well, since you shop for her, maybe you could sit in for her," I persisted.

"You wouldn't want me in one of your classes," he said, merriment returning to his eyes. "I was expelled from a metaphysics class once." He paused. "I peeked into the soul of the girl next to me."

I smiled at his joke.

"I took a speed reading course once." He waited until I dutifully said "oh?" before continuing, "but I had to stop because I ran into a bookmark."

"That's funny." By then we were again on opposite sides of the cash counter.

"Actually. It's Woody Allen," he confessed. Sensing a receptive audience, he went on as he handed over a ten dollar bill. "I haven't always been a fireman you know."

"No?" I'd bite.

"In my younger days I worked in a factory that made fire hydrants but I couldn't park anywhere near the place."

I laughed out loud as I handed him back his change. He lingered, casually leaning his hip against the counter. He was obviously delighted at a new audience. Maybe the guys at the firehall had heard all his jokes before. It was silly but I couldn't help it. I felt laughter bubbling up inside me. It was like trying to hold an ice cube under water. It was irrepressibly pushing upwards. It had been too long since I had laughed with an attractive man who tried to please me with a gift of humor.

"Maybe laughter is flirtatious," Grama suggested, and I went red in the face.

"You should be on a stage," I said to Daniel in self defense—well, it was all I could think of at the time—and we both chorused the old punchline, "There's one leaving in five minutes!"

"There's nothing like a good joke," Daniel said with a grin.

"And that was nothing like a good joke!" I replied with a laugh.

Daniel's grin grew broader. "I can take a hint." He raised up his hands in surrender. "I'm leaving." He looked straight into my eyes and I felt his blue eyes pierce right through me. "See you soon, Aggie." And then he was gone.

Hobbes continued to purr loudly in the silence and butted his head into my arm. I stroked him distractedly as I stared at the door, wondering.

A few minutes later I was still grinning foolishly, thinking of the twinkle in his eyes when Joyce came in to work. She eyed me curiously. She must have wondered what made the boss so giddy that morning. I guess I hadn't been very good company lately. After the hot and bothered time I'd been having since the town meeting, Daniel's humor was a welcome breath of cool air.

I wondered if everyone in this town had the habit of disappearing so abruptly, if everyone was a hit-and-run artist. First Jo, now Daniel.

SHORTLY AFTER LUNCH, I just finished cutting out my *Seven Sisters* fabrics when Jo called on the telephone.

"You did really well at the meeting last night," she said. "You fit right in, but then I thought you would. Everyone liked you a lot."

"I liked them, too," I answered sincerely.

"You got us all organized," she continued.

"Oh dear, I didn't mean to. I didn't intend to get so involved. I'm just so emotional about this issue, I got carried away. I don't know why this happens to me. When I get into a group of people, I end up running things, when all I want to do is volunteer and help out."

"Probably because you're a natural leader," Jo replied. "And you're passionate about this, shall we say, 'project'. Passion often brings out leadership in people."

"I've always thought of myself more as a sort of facilitator," I explained.

"I know, but leadership usually isn't about seeking glory. It's about simply getting something done. You're probably a good leader in spite of yourself," she continued. "Perhaps you should just relax and accept your role."

"Hmm. I don't know. Does anyone actually go around saying, 'I'm a leader, so follow me'?" I replied. "That would be like the guy who runs out in front of a parade, pretending to lead people who are already going somewhere!"

"Isn't he the same fella who says, 'Tell me where my people are going so I can lead them?' But seriously. Leadership is like stature. It's something which can only be conferred on you by others. You can work to acquire *status* by your own efforts, but *stature* is given to you by other people's opinion. Leadership is conferred upon you when people follow you."

"What does it takes to be a good leader?" I asked.

"I think probably the most important thing is being able to listen to people and really hear what they say. Being able to ask the right questions, like you were doing last night. You asked questions that got us moving. Sometimes posing the right questions is more effective than having all the answers. Asking key questions is crucial to transformation, and leadership is all about getting people to transform themselves, to change themselves in some way. Isn't that what you did in your counselling practice?"

"I suppose. I know I spent a great deal of time asking people, 'what do you want to have happen'. I never told them how or what to do. I used to ask, 'how can you make it happen?' I never thought of that as a leadership skill. I thought it was support and empowerment."

"And so what's the difference?" she challenged.

"Hmmm," I acknowledged her point.

"Of course being bossy helps too!" she laughed. "Sometimes you have to be able to tell people what to do, in the nicest possible way of course. We've needed a leader for the Wombats for some time now."

"But not me," I protested.

"Why not?"

"Well, I'm not old enough. You or Viola should be the leaders."

"Thanks a lot!" Jo laughed. "I think you just called me an old bag!"

"I didn't mean it that way!" I exclaimed, embarrassed.

"I know. That's okay," She passed off the joke. "Besides, I'm too busy. I haven't got the time for it. Time? Ha! I won't be around forever, you know." She sighed deeply. "In any case leadership isn't about age. Granted, wisdom does come with experience and for me it came late in life . . ."

I smiled as she unintentionally patted herself on the back.

". . . but wisdom has to come with a capable voice in order to be leadership. Age or seniority has nothing to do with it."

"You know, you talk about voices and it may sound crazy but I still hear Grama's voice in my head talking to me." I wasn't going to admit that I *saw* her as well. Like *Topper* the ghost, who only haunted one person, I was the only one Grama haunted. "To me she is still here, in my head." I tapped my temple even though Jo obviously couldn't see me over the telephone. "It's as if she's an old voice and I'm still listening to her." Grama could be the Wombat leader, I thought.

"That's good," Jo replied. "The older you get the more you should listen and talk to spirits. But you have to listen to the voices only until you become one yourself. I suspect there's a voice in you waiting to come out."

"But not everyone is supposed to become a leader," I argued. "Being the titular head of my family by age is not the same thing as being its true matriarch."

"Perhaps not," Jo agreed. "Do you remember the story of Jonah?"

"Not really," I said. Sunday School was a long time ago and like most people I only remembered he had been swallowed by a whale but I couldn't remember why.

Jo continued, "Jonah had been directed by God to go and teach the people of Ninevah, but whether he was afraid or just obstinate, he refused to go. Instead Jonah boarded a boat sailing in the opposite direction. Well, it wasn't long before a storm blew up and it threatened to capsize the boat and drown everyone on board. Jonah realized that this was God's punishment for his disobedience so he went to the captain and said, 'Throw me overboard. It's the only way you will all be saved.' But the captain took pity on Jonah and refused to throw him overboard. In the meantime the storm grew worse and Jonah again pleaded to be sacrificed—believing he had made a mistake which couldn't be corrected. That in itself is a bigger mistake. Finally everyone agreed that it was the only thing to do and they cast him overboard. Jonah ended up in the belly of the whale for three days. There he contemplated his error and eventually was spit up on shore. In the end he went to Ninevah after all. So what does it tell you?"

"The more you deny your destiny, the harder life becomes," I replied.

"So, don't you think that if a parade forms behind you, you'd better lead the band somewhere?"

"Touchè," I acquiesced.

"Anyway," she changed the subject. "Do you want to come to

the library with Viola and me? Marlene can't make it so she asked me to go for her."

"Sure, why not?" I hadn't had time to visit the library before now. Besides I admit to a certain curiosity about dusty old cellars and secret stuff locked away. We arranged to meet at ten thirty, when the library would open. When the time came, I left Joyce in charge. Then I walked the six blocks over to the vine-covered, red brick building. When I arrived, Jo and Viola were already inside, talking to the young librarian who sat behind a stack of books.

"Funny," the librarian said as I approached. "That's the second request I've had to see the old records, Mrs. Winterspoon. There was a young man here just last week," she addressed Viola, her former colleague.

Oh, oh. We all looked at each other.

That didn't sound good, I shook my head.

Viola took the keys from the librarian and led the way slowly to the creaky wooden stairs and the vault below. There was a smell of musty paper and dust in the storage room. A low ceiling meant we had to duck under rusty pipes. It was a closely packed room with shelves and filing cases jammed everywhere. There might have been an order to it once but obviously later caretakers had simply shoved in material in a pell mell fashion. Viola tut-tutted disdainfully as we tried to pick our way through. She obviously disapproved of how the new regime was operating since she had handed over the reins of power. It was like excavating an archeological dig. The air was close and stuffy and there was barely room for the three of us to move about. My hands were soon grimey. I'd certainly have to wash up before handling fabric again.

We finally located Viola's carefully catalogued box of files. It wasn't where she had left it, she said, which explained why it took so long to locate. She opened it slowly and sure enough, it was empty. The contents were gone. Vanished. Purloined! King Tut wasn't in his tomb. Someone beat us to the buried treasure.

We stared at the empty cardboard container. All of Viola's

meticulously filed records and documents pertaining to the history of the Armbruster Building were missing.

"You don't think Little Al stole them, do you?" Viola naively asked.

"Of course," replied Jo glumly.

"But how could he be that devious?" I objected.

"I told you, he's not too bright," she responded.

"But couldn't he be arrested?"

"Well, no, not really. It would be his word against the librarian's. Besides, it's only library material, for Pete's sake. He'd probably just get a slap on the wrist and a fine, since no one cared about the material anyway."

"I suppose it's up in smoke now," I sighed. Jo nodded gravely.

We drove the few blocks back to the shop in Jo's bright red Volkswagen Beetle. Lady Bug, she called it. It had been over twenty-five years since I sat in the back seat of one of those funny little cars. I wanted to resurrect some happy memories of Jack and me and our innocent backseat days at college, but I was too distracted to enjoy the ride. Besides, Jo drove like a red bat out of hell. I couldn't tell whether it was because she was angry or because she did everything at breakneck speed. I wouldn't have thought you could get a Beetle to turn a corner on two wheels . . .

Remarkably, we parked without incident. Jo walked over to Ivy's restaurant and Viola and I returned to my shop. Viola sat rocking in Grama's chair while I reported the bad news to Marlene and Millie by telephone. Marlene wasn't surprised. Maybe working in the same office as Al Junior she'd seen how he operated in the cut-and-thrust business of real estate. Millie was upset and appalled at the loss of the papers, but when I repeated the librarian's comment and intimated that Al Junior might have had something to do with it, she was adamant that he couldn't possibly have been involved. We'll probably never know, I thought as I hung up the telephone.

A few minutes later Jo came back into the shop smiling and

shaking her head. "Ivy said, 'Just because one souffle falls, don't give up, we've got more eggs,'" she recounted.

"Yeah, I know," I nodded wearily. "But this was our nice, big ostrich egg, you know."

She nodded and waved and made a chin-up gesture as she held out her hand to Viola, ready to take her home.

IT HAD BEEN A HECTIC COUPLE OF WEEKS and by Sunday I was so tired of tea, toast and take-away that I decided to treat myself to a decent meal at The Quilt Inn. I found out that the owners, Gail and Michael, had both left corporate jobs to follow their dream of running a country inn, and they had faced all the difficulties and uncertainties which that entailed. They converted the inn from a rambling old farmhouse of stone and timber beams. The gardens and orchard provided them with the delicious fresh produce they served. Over the years I had been to the inn a couple of times and had always admired the wonderful quilts on display throughout the rooms and halls. With its green lawns and lovely old shade trees, the inn was a peaceful setting to unwind in.

After a delicious brunch of Eggs Benedict and fresh squeezed orange juice on the patio, I rambled back into the main hall. And there I saw the quilt hanging on a wall. I had to stop in my tracks to stare at it, it was so wonderful. The quilt was small, not quite four feet square. It was bright and bold with scintillating colors like flames which leapt around the design. It was a very raw and energetic tapestry. Awkward in its design and even poorly executed in some places, it was utterly captivating in the emotion it expressed. There was pain in it, but it was full of life and movement. It was as if there was agony in the quilt, yet joy in the quilter.

I was overcome with curiosity.

"Gail, this is marvellous," I exclaimed when she came into the room. "You have to tell me about this quilt."

"I thought you'd be interested in it. There's a fascinating story behind it."

"Tell me. I'm all ears."

"You wouldn't remember the terrible MacPherson fire."

I shook my head, no. But as soon as she said the word "fire" I knew that that was what I'd been seeing in the quilt. There is nothing so alive as fire, or so terrifying and deadly at the same time. Looking at the quilt reminded me of staring at a campfire on a pitch black night. When you look away from the fire you can't see anything else for a long time, until your eyes readjust. When I looked away from it, the quilt seemed to remain emblazoned on my inner eye. I immediately wondered if this was a memory quilt for someone who had died in the fire.

"It was before you came to town, about a year and a half ago," she explained. "The MacPhersons lived with their three kids in a wood frame house over on Dalton Street. Jessie and Tom had a reputation for partying it up and they often left their kids alone in the house—"

Gail told me the grim tale. A fire broke out in the home one night when the children were alone. One of the off-duty local firemen heard the call go out over his two-way truck radio. He was close to the address but he didn't have any fire-fighting equipment with him. He went there anyway and was the first to arrive at the scene. The house was already engulfed in flames. Without a second thought he plunged into the burning building which collapsed behind him as he made his way to the back bedroom where the children were. He broke the window and pushed the two older children out. By the time he rescued the youngest both he and the baby were on fire themselves. He rolled himself and the child on the ground to extinguish the flames. Everyone was watching the front of the house, not the back where they were. With the baby in his smoldering arms, eventually he staggered to the front of the house where help was waiting. Within minutes the entire house was burned to the ground but the three children were saved.

It was a horrific story but one of fearless courage and compassion.

"As it turned out," Gail continued, "the fireman's hands were terribly burned and he had to undergo extensive rehabilitation. One of his nurses was a quilter and she taught him to quilt as a way to get flexibility and strength back into his fingers. This was his first quilt. I talked him into letting me hang it up for a while. He doesn't tell anyone about his quilting. I knew you, more than anyone, would appreciate it."

"I'm amazed." I was enthusiastic and curious. "What was his name?"

"Daniel," Gail replied. "Daniel—"

And then I remembered the fireman's hands. "Fairbanks," I interrupted.

"You know him?"

"I met him," I replied. "I remember his hands."

"Of course," Gail nodded.

I didn't tell her I also remembered his full-of-life sense of humor.

So my strange male "customer," fireman Daniel Fairbanks, was indeed the quilter after all. And he was the hero.

I stood looking at Daniel's quilt and wondered about the heart of a man who could produce such a raw and intense and vital work of art, and love. This was passion, which sometimes burns intensely like fire. Yet fire is also terrifying. It's organic and primal. We instinctively push away from it, shield ourselves from it. It is a rare hero who plunges into the flames that would melt an angel's wings. What makes a man commit his body to saving the lives of others? What makes an artist commit his pain and experience to creativity? In this case there was a private person not even looking for accolades or praise.

Then I remembered his joke and smiled. Indeed, looking at Daniel's firey quilt, I had peeked into his metaphysical soul. I blushed at the intimacy.

I seem to keep crossing paths with this mysterious man, I thought and wondered when I would see him again. I was even more intrigued than before.

OVER THE WEEKS I had begun to establish an almost daily routine. Morning coffee in the upstairs bay window, open the shop, chat with customers, take my lunch at Ivy's on rainy days or in the park on sunny ones, do the afternoon banking, close the shop and retire upstairs for whatever passed as dinner. On the clear evenings I took a walk around the town, in a different direction each time, finding my way on foot, exploring. Then, when the sun had set, I would return home and descend to the shop by way of the back staircase and sit sewing my quilt blocks under the lamp, with Hobbes as my sleepy companion.

Throughout June we began our campaign to save the town square. One good thing happened early: my daughter Susan came "home" again from college for the Summer. Grama's Quilt Shop was doing well enough that I could hire her parttime and she enjoyed working with the customers. It also gave her a chance and an excuse to start another quilt. Being a teacher-in-training helped her land another parttime job at a local children's camp. I had a hunch she'd be writing about the experience and would end up with another children's storybook. If she weren't so intent on being a teacher, Susan would be a good writer. She collects stories like some people collect stamps. Every night she makes long entries in a private journal which she keeps on her bedside table. She knows that I would never read it without her permission but I asked her once what she was writing about.

"Oh, you know, Mom, just stuff." She shrugged at first, embarrassed at revealing herself. "I write down things that happen to me sometimes, but mostly I like to write down the things that happen to other people, the stories they tell me about their lives. And about how I feel about people." She shook her blond head and brushed her hair back. "I just think people are so fascinating. I don't want to forget anything—"

See what I mean?

Naturally, Susan immediately took an active part in our campaign, and offered to help with the petition. As the days heated up, so did the town. We all had a copy of the petition and it went everywhere with us as we campaigned for signatures. The petition presented a counter-proposal to answer the redevelopment project. It asked people to support a new one-way traffic flow around the park, with angle parking, and a renovation for the existing buildings, and it asked them to support a plan to renew the use of the park, saving the old trees, and attracting tourists. We didn't mention the historic Armbruster building at all. Without the Preservation Order, it wasn't a good ploy anymore. We did put forward the suggestion to sell bricks for new footpaths in the park.

The Wombats attended the last meeting of the local Women's Business Association—it was the full group with some seventy members—before its Summer recess. Susan had offered to officially address the meeting during the any-other-business segment. I was relieved not to have to make a speech myself. I hate public speaking, it's a near-death experience for me. Susan did an excellent job of asking for the businesswomen's support for our cause. She appealed to their sense of injustice and economics. She was sensible and logical in her plea and was roundly applauded afterward.

During the mix and mingle portion of the meeting we lobbied the members individually about our alternative proposal. It was no real surprise to find out that not everyone was nostalgic and supportive of the town square. Some opposed saving it outright— for economic reasons or just for modernism. I could understand that. Some were indifferent. That I couldn't understand. I've never understood the attitude that if it isn't in my backyard or threatening my family directly, I don't have to think about it. The world has a strange way of shrinking over time and eventually "over there" does end up in our yard. Another delusion of insignificance—we think we are so small that some of the dust won't hit us when we turn on the fan.

In the end, enough of the members were interested, inspired and motivated to form a committee to help raise funds. They chose a slogan, STOP, Save The Old Park, which we liked. And then they adjourned for the Summer. Suddenly it was all over.

Officially, they would help again in the Fall—if we still had a park by then. They didn't seem to realize the urgency of the situation. Couldn't they see that this was their town we were talking about, I railed inwardly.

After all the rhetoric, it would be up to a few individuals to keep things going during the summer. I was disappointed but it was understandable. I already knew that the association was a fairly disparate and essentially non-political group. It underlined the difficulty of organizing a group of people to take a stand against something. I had to remind myself of my own advice to the Wombats about it being easier to convince people to support something they like, than to take a stand against something they don't like. If this was going to be typical of the response we would receive, we were in big trouble.

Obviously, if we were to win supporters, we would have to be stronger in presenting our counter-proposal. On the way home I asked myself, why it is that the issues in life which we try desperately to ignore tend to keep coming back and slapping us in the face until we deal with them?

THE NEXT DAY I TELEPHONED JO and admitted I had made a mistake.

"Before you say it, I know. I should have spoken myself, shouldn't I?" I confessed.

"Yes," she agreed.

"This isn't Susan's fight. It's mine. I shouldn't have abrogated my responsibility in speaking up," I continued. There is a natural time in life to pass on the reins to the next generation and it's a mistake to hold on too long, I knew. But it's also a mistake to hand them over too soon—my daughters' shoulders aren't strong enough and I am not yet weak enough to give up my responsibilities—just because I am tired, or literally afraid to stand up and make a speech. Even when I knew I was called to speak up, I couldn't always find the courage to do so. Fear too often silences us. But the silence won't protect us from the truth. Or the consequences.

"Yes," she said.

"Making the best use of resources and deploying the right person for the job, including myself, is a leadership quality, isn't it?" I concluded unhappily.

"Don't be too hard on yourself. The fact that you can take corrective action means you are still a good leader. Leadership is a role you grow into, like any other, by making mistakes."

"The reality is, I was afraid. I'm so uncomfortable making speeches," I admitted.

"I can understand that. But all you have to do is speak from the heart. Tell it like it is. Let your passion carry you forward and it will carry others forward too. Your passion will persuade. That's all it is—a sales job."

"Sales?" I protested. "I'm not a salesperson." Jo tends to think everything is related to business.

Jo laughed. "Oh yes, you are! Everyone is, because, inevitably, every single relationship is about sales. If you're in business, you are in sales. And if you're in politics, honey, you're really in sales! If you've ever tried to get your kids to bed at night, you're in sales. Sales is simply persuasion. You want to persuade someone to agree with your point of view or to take an action you want them to take. If you are passionate about anything you automatically become a salesman for that passion. Without a sale there is no passion; without passion there is no sale. Every time you try to persuade anyone, you are selling. Did you ever try to convince Jack to buy a new piece of furniture?"

I laughed. "You bet. Of course."

"There you go. That's sales!" she continued. "The thing to remember is that people buy benefits, not features. A person doesn't buy a red car or a blue blouse. A person buys how the car or blouse makes them feel. The color is the feature, how they feel is the benefit. For example, you say, 'This car is undercoated *which means* you will have carefree maintenance for a long time and you will save money.' Likewise, you have to sell this proposal on the benefits it will bring to people. How good it will make them feel."

"That's great! That's exactly what I needed to know," I exclaimed, suddenly excited. "As always you have great advice, Jo. I'm okay with persuasion—shoot, I was married for fourteen years, I've done that hundreds of times. If all I have to do is point out the benefits then that's easy. But when I think of selling anything I still picture pushy, foot-in-door salesmen."

"I know what you're saying. Most people have a notion of salespeople as the snake oil salesmen who traveled the wild West, bilking the innocent pioneers."

I told her how the Council meeting and watching Little Al Junior reminded me of the move *The Rainmaker*.

"But salesmanship these days is much more sophisticated and less aggressive than that." Jo explained. "The fact is, most people sell themselves. If the idea meets the customer's needs, they will buy it. If it doesn't meet their needs, no amount of persuasion will create a sale. Like the movie, *The Rainmaker*. It's always been a favorite of mine. Starbuck, the Burt Lancaster character, seemed to be a con man. But what he sold was not rain, it was hope, and dreams, and believing in yourself. That's what Katharine Hepburn, the plain and cynical Lizzie character, bought. She had a need for dreams and possiblity in her life. She needed to believe in herself. It's a very powerful movie."

"Until now I had a different view of it, I guess. I'm going to think about what you said. It all makes sense. I think I can be comfortable with this," I replied.

"Good for you, honey," she said brusquely. "Now, I gotta go see the doctor."

"Anything wrong?" I asked.

"No. He just likes to listen to my heart every once in a while to make sure it's still ticking!" She laughed. "Talk to you later."

We rang off but I did think about her words. That evening I rented a copy of *The Rainmaker* and watched it again, with a different view than before. In the end, I decided I had to reconsider my attitude toward what I was doing, in my business and in my life, and how I could apply this to saving the downtown. Never again would I back down from speaking the truth. It wasn't a redevelopment counter-proposal I was selling, I realized. It was a vision of Clareville.

The next day, just before closing time, the telephone rang. It was Daniel.

"Hi there!" he said cheerfully.

"Hi yourself." I was pleased to hear from him.

"I hear you're involved with the group trying to save the downtown."

"Yes," I confirmed, "but I'm not too sure about it. Fortunately, I'm working with lots of friends." I wanted to ask him about the quilt but felt it was too much of an intrusion.

"Can I help at all?" he asked. "I signed your petition, but is there anything else I can do?"

My mind raced. "Well, I don't know. Everyone's got their assignments—"

"Well, good. But, would you like my phone number?"

That was strange. The moment's hesitation on the telephone said we had both been taken aback by his question. He spluttered, "I mean, in case I can help. Anything at all. I'm on nights this week so I'll give you that number too." He paused and then recited his numbers. "Oh, and I have a new car phone with an answering machine. If you call it says, 'Sorry but I'm home right now and can't take your call. Leave a message and I'll call you when I go out.'"

I laughed.

"You have a great laugh," Daniel said quietly, "Like a little bell ringing," he added in a soft voice. A pause went by—but I didn't know what to say. Maybe if I'd said something the conversation would have gone a different way. But the moment passed. He cleared his throat and then added more matter-of-factly, "Speaking of my car, I got stopped for speeding the other day."

What happened?" I chuckled in anticipation in spite of myself.

"The cop said I was doing ninety in a fifty mile per-hour zone. I told him I didn't plan to be out that long."

This time, I definitely guffawed. His jokes all were so silly, but I guess I just needed to laugh.

"No more," I begged. "Thank you, Daniel. Thanks for cheering me up. Call anytime."

"I will," he said with a strange earnest emphasis and rang off.

"You okay?" Joyce asked with a curious smile but I waved her off.

I was puzzled by my schoolgirl reaction to his humor. Maybe I was so strung out, it was simply hysteria. I felt flattered, nevertheless at the same time I also began to question if he ever did anything but tell jokes. That could get on your nerves, I thought unkindly. Maybe he doesn't know how to have an adult conversation. The refrain from the Peggy Lee song *Is That All There Is* started to run through my head.

"Humor is sexy," I heard Grama reminding me. "People who joke well together, stroke well together."

"Oh, pu-lease!" I grimaced. "It's also a defence mechanism," I grumbled, "which people use to avoid intimacy."

Daniel's joking reminded me of a comic skit I'd seen many years ago. A famous impersonator constantly talks in the voice of Cary Grant or other romantic characters. Even offstage with his girlfriend. She's amused and flattered for a while but eventually she tells him that she wants to really get to know him, that he doesn't have to always use other men's voices. He resists but eventually she persuades him that she loves him and he should trust her and just be himself. They're sitting on a couch. He pauses for a minute and thinks and then starts to talk about baseball cards and frogs and other stuff young boys talk about. Slowly a look of horror crosses her face as he rambles on. She realizes that she's gotten exactly what she asked for—and that his "true" personality had frozen when he was twelve, when he had learned to mimic famous men instead of developing his own mature identity. The skit ended when, suddenly inspired, she taps him on the shoulder and says, "Excuse me. Could I please speak to Cary Grant!"

Could I please speak to the real Daniel Fairbanks?

Be careful what you ask for. If he weren't telling jokes, who would I end up talking to? Be grateful for the ray of sunshine he offers, I advised myself. I tried to put it out of my mind but I was flushed from laughter, embarrassment, and confusion. My hand instinctively went to the chain at my neck. I unclasped it and flipped open the heart-shaped locket. "Lock in the good times," Jack used to say. There we were, Jack and I, younger, dark-haired, full of hope and confidence. A whole quarter of a century ago, locked in time. There was my Jack, tanned, smiling and with a deep love in his eyes. Frozen and immortal, he would never change, never age. Until death do us part. I suppose as far as he was concerned I was still Jack's wife. Death only ends the bodily marriage, not the love, not the intention.

I had to look away.

By then it was time to close the shop. Joyce had rung out the cash register and tidied up. She was ready to leave so I waved good-night to her. I closed the locket and clasped the chain securely around my neck again.

I turned out the lights and slipped the front door chain through the hasp and snapped the lock firmly shut.

I had to close the door.

SUSAN AND I WERE PERCHED on stools at the cutting table that evening, reviewing our campaign and planning strategies when Jennifer walked into the shop. I was so surprised, you could have knocked me over with a feather.

"What are you doing here!" I exclaimed, hugging and kissing her.

"This is just NOT my day, Mom," she laughed, exasperated "In fact it hasn't been my week, to be exact!"

"Are you alright?" I asked, now worried.

"Yeah, I'm okay. I've been fired."

"Oh no," we intoned.

"And I broke up with Jim," she continued, on the verge of tears.

"Oh dear," we chorused. I wasn't totally surprised by that news.

"And if that wasn't bad enough, I got a flat tire just outside town," she sighed. "This is just not my day."

"Poor baby," I consoled. "When did all this happen? Why didn't you call? Why didn't you say anything? Come and tell us all about it."

"Well, it sounded like you had your own troubles. I didn't want to worry you, but now—" she trailed off mournfully.

For the next hour Jennifer wailed out all the details of how she'd been called into the boss's office and told about the company downsizing, and her arguments with Jim and their final break-up. She finally had had too much togetherness and just made up her mind to leave, even though it was painful to do so. And then when she decided to jump in her car and come home for some reassurance, she'd had a flat tire. Like the chorus in a Greek tragedy we moaned and commiserated with her. She was hurt, angry, frustrated and sad all at the same time, and the only thing we could do was listen.

"So, what happened?" she finally railed. "I thought I was supposed to be rewarded for living a good life? I was honest and hardworking and committed but look what happened. I'm so angry I could spit! Sure, everyone said it wasn't my fault, downsizing was purely a financial decision on the part of management. But that's not how it felt. I didn't have enough seniority—that was unfair. There are others who were kept on who didn't do half the work I did. I hadn't complained about any job they asked me to do. I worked extra hours and never even put in for overtime pay. It isn't fair!" She pounded on the table.

"I know how you feel, baby," I put my arm around her. There was so little I could say. I would have had to admit I had been feeling the same way too lately.

"Mom, sometimes I think Grama got it all wrong. She said if you build a good strong character, live with integrity and take an active role in life, you'll be successful."

"Grama never said it would be easy," I pointed out.

"But nothing seems to be working. Everything is going wrong.

Even for you here in Clareville," she welded her misery to mine. "Look at what's happened to your shop. You start a new business and then, boom, suddenly it could be taken away from you like that." She snapped her fingers. "When does the struggle end?" she sighed.

"The only good thing that happened," Jennifer said, finally winding down, "Was when my tire blew, a good-looking guy in a sportscar stopped to change it for me. He was really cute." She brightened slightly. That's my Jennifer, I thought, even in her darkest despair, the tiniest rainbow will perk her up. Even as a baby she could be easily cajoled out of a tantrum.

"One door closes and another opens," Susan remarked, smiling.

"Oh no!" Jennifer protested. "He was nice, that's all. There's no way I'm getting involved with anybody again for a LONG time. Besides I think I knew all along that it wouldn't work out with Jim. We were just too different but I didn't want to see it. Anyway, I'm really more angry about losing my job than about Jim. I put my whole life into that job."

"Maybe that's why you broke up with Jim," Susan suggested. "Remember what Grama used to say about choices. Sometimes you have to give up one thing to pour yourself, heart and soul, into another."

"I didn't mean it that way," Jennifer replied huffily. "I meant that with Jim I could see the end coming and was prepared for it but with my job, it was a total surprise. Maybe I wouldn't feel so bad if it hadn't been so unexpected. It just wasn't fair," Jennifer repeated her complaint.

"Ah, 'fair,'" I mused. "What's 'fair,' Jen? How do you measure these things? If you hadn't stopped with a flat tire but had then driven on into an accident, would that have been fair? How is God supposed to know how you are going to view events and mete them out to you accordingly?" I raised my eyebrows to emphasize the rhetorical question.

Jennifer looked at me annoyed, as though she wasn't receiving the sympathy she felt she deserved.

"I guess that's the disadvantage of being young," Susan continued, philosophically. "We expect life to be fair. I suppose when you get old you realize it isn't always fair. You just want it to be anything, so long as it's life."

"Well, I don't accept that. That's giving up," Jennifer sniffed. "*Grama* would never recommend giving up." Jennifer looked at me but directed her comment at Susan.

"It isn't giving up, it's simply not fighting what is," I replied. "Acceptence isn't giving up. Life is neither fair nor unfair, it just is."

"But I don't like it the way it is," Jennifer argued.

"It doesn't matter whether you like it or not," I said gently. "That's all there is."

Jennifer looked glum. Susan touched her arm gently and quoted Grama, "For things to change, first I must change." We all fell silent.

I looked at my two daughters and wondered how they could be so unalike and yet so much the same. And I wondered who had the right approach. Jennifer is a fighter. Susan is an acquiescer. On the constantly moving quicksand of life, they have different survival strategies. Jennifer tries to take a rigid stand on the moving ground, forcing it to conform to her wishes, hoping her powerful determination can withstand every adversity. On the other hand, Susan takes a deep breath and lets it engulf her, hoping she can hold her breath long enough, until it all passes by. But anyone who ever watched Tarzan movies on Saturday morning knows that the only way out of quicksand is not to struggle against it but to relax and float with it.

"So what was the guy like who fixed your tire?" Susan asked, pointedly changing the subject.

"He was really cute. He asked me out," Jennifer admitted with a sigh. "But I said no. As I said, I don't want to get involved with anyone else."

"Honey, it's only dinner." I smiled at her drama.

She ignored my interruption. "And certainly not in this hick town. I'm not staying here. I'm going back to the city as soon as possible!"

"I guess it would be too much of a challenge to stay here. Too scary," Susan commented off-handedly.

"Scary? Here in Mudville? It's the city that's scary," Jennifer replied sharply.

"But here in Mudville as you call it, you're wide open to people. You're visible. You have to be yourself and you can't hide in anonymity like you can in the city," Susan provoked. Sometimes sisters don't know when to quit.

"You could be a real pain in the neck if you worked at it, you know," Jennifer snapped.

"You're upset," Susan told Jennifer. "Someone threw a monkey wrench into your plans and it hurts. I understand. I'm sorry I ruffled your feathers," she said with sudden gentleness. I was struck by the maturity and compassion in her voice.

"I'm sorry," Jennifer mumbled her apology as she slumped over the cutting table and dropped her head sadly onto her folded arms. Susan got up to make tea and patted Jennifer's arm consolingly as she passed by, and the three of us spent a long night talking.

WHEN DOES THE STRUGGLE end? I heard Jennifer's voice ringing in my ears as I lay staring sleeplessly at the ceiling. I wished I could tell her that it does end. I could appreciate exactly how she felt. As Susan said, you take a step forward and someone throws a monkey wrench into the works. I guess that should be my next quilt block, I sighed. Some quilter somewhere must have experienced that sudden collision of chaos with her intention and designed a quilt block called *Monkey Wrench.* Quilters have been making that block ever since. It isn't particularly pretty, although it is deceptively easy, so it must be because the name evokes an experience we have all shared.

Monkey Wrench. I don't even know where the expression comes from but it's appropriate. Einstein once said, "God doesn't play dice." He was saying something about fate and probabilities and the fact that the Universe can be counted on to behave in a normal manner. But for me, somehow it seemed "the gods" were throwing dice on our fate, throwing a wrench into the works. One day we were up, the next we were down. Like rolling around on the wheel of life. So, it isn't that the struggle never ends. It's that it is inexorably recurring.

Up: I had met some wonderful women who were a boon to my adventure. We had a great plan. Down: We lost the Armbruster papers. Up: Susan was home lending a hand. Down: The businesswomen's association wasn't going to help us. Then there was Jennifer and her latest troubles. There were the daily ups and downs of the quilt shop business which I continued to struggle with. And what to do about Daniel? I couldn't even begin to think about that.

Yet every time I felt completely disheartened something came along to raise me up again. Perhaps the problem is that the monkey wrenches seem to come along swiftly and unexpectedly, but it feels as though the boons are slower to appear, harder to recognize.

Jennifer had challenged Grama's values. She assumed that simply becoming the right person and living with integrity solved all of life's problems. Grama had given us the best of her wisdom. Her lessons were about being-ness in life. It was a solid foundation but it was up to us to discover the doing-ness, to travel the path of action and engaging the world. It doesn't mean we'll never get lost—the pressures and confusion of everyday living sometimes makes us forget our way. Grama's lessons were simply the compass which always points to true north—the means to find the way home.

So what was keeping me going, I puzzled. How could I help Jennifer?

I searched the shadowy ceiling for a long time before I finally realized that the answer was passion. I thought about the wheel of life. If you sit at the center or hub of the wheel you are safe and remain in a motionless tranquility, but that's not how you're supposed to engage the world. Saying a passionate "yes" and partici-pating in life means you take the leap of faith out to the flying rim of the wheel where you find yourself on the up and down cycles of experience. Saying "yes" takes courage, and holding on to the spinning wheel takes courage.

In an abstract sort of way, the *Monkey Wrench* block looks like a squared wheel that would certainly give a person a rough ride. If the pioneers had had square wheels on their covered wagons we'd all still be sitting in New Jersey! Metaphorically, they did have square wheels, and yet we're not in New Jersey. It was their passion to move forward into the challenge which kept them going despite their "Kansas troubles." It's passion that gives us the strength to endure the bumps and inevitable chaos on the open road, or more importantly when there is no road.

I decided to make my background for this simple block brown like the earth that the covered wagons traveled across. The "wheel" became blue and grey for the skies overhead that alternate be-tween fair and foul. There are times when I still feel as though I'm riding in a cart with square wheels. Passion alone doesn't solve all the problems. It's just the fuel which keeps us going. Just because we find allies in life doesn't mean the journey is over. There is still a lot to be done. Alone. Sometimes I'm still a lone square wheel bumping down the dusty road.

SIX

Tangled Briars

JENNIFER'S WHEEL OF LIFE STOPPED, for the moment at least, in Clareville. Despite her protests that she would be heading back to the city as soon as possible, she settled into small town living fairly easily. I was pleased to have both my girls back under my roof again. Mostly. It was a much smaller roof than we had been used to, and I found that I had really enjoyed having my own space for the first time in twenty-five years. However, once we established some house rules and a bathroom schedule, my cozy little upstairs apartment was pretty comfortable for the three of us. And Hobbes, of course. Although when the women became too much for him he could always retreat to his window view in the shop below.

Every day Jennifer continued an active job search in the city. But she also quickly involved herself in the town square drama. It was her cup of tea. It had hot words and strong feelings on both sides and it gave a certain air of excitement to her view of an otherwise ho-hum small town. Helping me was an excuse to go out and meet people and as a result she started making friends. Apparently she was having a good time because she often came home whistling and looking pleased with herself. I found out from Susan that she happened to run into the young man who had changed her flat tire and he had asked her out again. I like persistence in Jennifer's young men. They'll need it. She agreed to have dinner with him next week. As Grama used to say, "Never say never, you just never know. . . ." So I guess Mudville was looking up.

One evening in July Susan and I went to watch Ivy's softball team play at the high school diamond. The sky had been blue and cloudless all day and it stayed hot until the sun dipped below the line of tall trees which bordered the schoolyard. I was surprised that so many people turned up. There were a lot of parents and friends of the players. It was a lively game, already in the third inning when we arrived. The opposing team from Chesterfield was being roundly booed at every play. But it was good-natured heckling. Even the umpire looked as though he was having fun. At least nobody had wanted to kill him yet.

There was a rather rowdy bunch of men on the far side of the diamond but for the most part they behaved themselves. I looked over at one point and suddenly spotted Daniel sitting among them. He was wearing a Detroit Tigers baseball hat, a t-shirt and bluejeans. Just as soon as I registered that it was him and said the word "Daniel" in my head, he looked up, straight at me. How does that happen? I looked away. Perhaps he hadn't seen me, I sort of hoped. With Susan sitting beside me I didn't want to draw his attention. I usually don't talk to my children about my men friends until there is something to say. With most of them there had been nothing to say. There's something odd about teenagers and their parents dating at the same time. It's somehow embarrassing. We're supposed to be waiting up for them, not the other way round.

I kept my head turned to the game but carefully watched him from the corner of my eye under the brim of my "Ivy's League" cap. He continued to joke and laugh with his buddies but after several minutes he put down his drink, leaned over and said something and then stood up, making his way down the bleachers to the front.

I heard Grama's voice again. "Heads up!" she called from the dugout. "Here he comes!"

Daniel walked over and stood leaning against the chain-link fence, waiting politely until the end of the inning. As the field changed, he turned and climbed up the end of the bleachers to the middle row where we were sitting, then he edged along toward me as people shuffled out of the way to make room for him.

"Hi, Aggie," he said as he sat down. It was obvious he intended to stay.

"Oh hello, Daniel," I replied in my best surprised-to-see-you-here voice.

"You like baseball? I thought you were a football fan."

"No. I'm into non-contact sports," I said, trying to make light of the situation. Oh, that was stupid, I realized.

"Really?" He laughed but left it alone.

On the other side of me Susan leaned forward and said, "Hi."

"This is my daughter, Susan. Susan, Daniel Fairbanks."

"Nice to meet you." He reached across me and shook her hand. I caught the scent of his cologne again and it unnerved me. It seemed too personal a thing to smell him up close like that.

A bat cracked and our attention was drawn back to the game. A high fly ball was hit left of center and a young blond girl ran backwards to catch it. "Yes!" we all chorused triumphantly as she caught it, then groaned as she fumbled the ball. The runner on third made a dash for home, scoring a run.

"Oh, too bad," Daniel remarked. "She'll kick herself later about that one. Christie usually has better hands than that."

"You know her?" I asked. "Oh, you probably know everybody in town."

He nodded yes. "She's Doc Smiley's daughter. Known her since she was a baby. She, too, is going to be a doctor some day."

"Hope she's not going to be a surgeon," Susan joked and then said, "Mom, I'm going to go sit with Sasha, okay?" Sasha was a counsellor at the camp where Susan worked.

"Sure, honey." Obviously she had decided to leave Daniel and me alone.

It turned out to be a pleasant evening. Outside in the fresh air Daniel was more relaxed and in his own element. Jeans and a t-shirt looked good on him. They gave him a cuddly masculine look. He looked confident and secure, not so intimidated as he had in the fabric shop. I realized he must have felt pretty foolish in there sometimes, among all that woman stuff. Daniel in the lion's den, I thought with a smile. It probably took a lot of courage to pursue his interest in quilting. We chatted casually between plays. As if he'd read my mind, he didn't tell any jokes. It was a real conversation, albeit punctuated with comments on the game. He asked about my children, my job and moving to Clareville. I tried to give him my life story in two-hundred words or less.

"And what about you?" I asked in turn. "Do you have family here?"

"Not really. Divorce. No kids." He shrugged his shoulders evasively.

I didn't know what else to ask. I guess if there are no children in a divorce it's hard to pursue that line of questioning. Besides I didn't want to be too pushy.

"Except your mother," I pointed out.

"Oh, yeah, right. Mother." Daniel stared studiously out into the playing field.

"I had brunch at The Quilt Inn last week," I said.

"Hmm?" he replied without taking his eyes off the game. He shifted uneasily in his seat.

"I saw the quilt you made."

"Oh." He looked down at his hands self-consciously.

"It's really beautiful, Daniel," I said softly. "It took my breath away."

With that Daniel looked at me and smiled with delight. "You really like it?" he asked like a big open-faced child seeking assurance. "I guess for a first quilt it's okay." He shrugged off-handedly.

"It's great," I assured him. "And what you did... you know, the fire . . . that was really extraordinary, really brave."

"Nah." He shrugged again, dissembling the praise. "It's my job."

He obviously felt embarrassed by the attention, so I tried to lighten the conversation. "So, it isn't your Mom who needs the quilting supplies . . ."

"No," he admitted sheepishly. "She died seven years ago."

"Then it's a good thing you didn't sign her up for one of my classes!"

We both laughed at that and let the conversation drift away to other topics. We were testing each other out in a pre-date dance, looking for points of interest, commonality which could carry us forward. The game played on until the streetlights came on and the floodlights lit up the playing field. The bats thwacked, feet pounded the dirt, and the ball whomped into worn leather gloves puncturing the twilight with carefree summer pleasure. A blue and not yet purple darkness surrounded us in the bleachers. Night bugs buzzed in the warm, still air.

During the seventh inning stretch Daniel went to the concession stand and bought us hotdogs and colas. As he passed his group of friends, a couple of remarks were called out to him. He stopped to make some comments himself and laughed but then waved them off and continued on his way.

At the end of the game the crowd began to disappear immediately. There was a sudden and scurried exodus to the parking lot. Daniel lingered. Susan headed toward me.

"Say Aggie. Maybe we could have dinner sometime," he suggested quickly with a smile.

Who could resist those blue eyes, I thought. "That would be very nice," I answered sincerely.

"Great. How about Saturday night? Being one of the few single guys at the firehall I don't get many weekends off, but if that's okay . . ."

"Sure. That would be great." I hoped I didn't sound too desperate or dateless.

"You close at six on Saturday. Can I pick you up at seven?"

"Fine," I confirmed as I started to climb over the seats to where Susan was waiting for me. "See you," I called out. Daniel made his way back to where some of his friends were still standing around talking.

"*Who* was that!" Susan demanded playfully when we got back into the car.

"Oh, just a guy who comes into the shop once in a while," I replied, trying to sound nonchalant.

"Nice eyes," she commented. Susan has my taste in men. She likes laughter and intelligence. Jennifer goes for Armani suits and "buns".

"Yeah," I agreed.

"But his hands."

"He's a fireman." I explained about the MacPherson fire, but not about Daniel's quilting. That could stay our secret, for now.

Susan watched me carefully as I spoke, and seemed satisfied that I didn't appear too interested in Daniel to warrant further comment.

As THE WEEKS OF SUMMER PASSED, we worked on our counter-proposal. Once the petition was drafted, it was mostly just a case of rallying support. "Just," ha!

Susan and Marlene designed a logo for our Save The Old Park slogan. It was shaped like a traffic stopsign only in green with three stylized trees on it. Instead of the familiar red diagonal line crossing the background, it had a big red checkmark saying "yes" to the trees. We printed flyers and handed them out outside the grocery stores. We slipped them under windshield wipers in parking lots. We stapled them to telephone poles. We couldn't afford to run ads, but Jo inveigled the editor of The Clareville Banner to write a couple of favorable articles encouraging keeping the old downtown. Unfortunately, a week later Councillor Frank Dempsey wrote a letter to the Editor that savaged our ideas. To which Marlene said, "Don't worry about it. That man's had a two-by-four up his keester for years. Nobody pays him no mind." We canvassed the small strip malls and talked to people about the proposal. Some days were heartening when positive responses were received. Some days were tough. And unfortunately, the public seemed to tire of the issue quickly, and wanted to move on to something else. There was bored annoyance in some responses. As the country song goes, "Some days are diamonds, some days are stone."

One afternoon as I was straightening bolts of fabric, a long dark shadow caught the corner of my eye. I looked up to see a lanky, hook-nosed, straw-haired old man step through the shop door. He looked all the world like Ichabod Crane in greasy overalls.

"Hello, M'am," he said politely, rubbing his hands on the sides of his pants. "My name is Horace Baker. I work in the garage over there on Wood Street." He turned and pointed across the park.

"Hello," I nodded with recognition. The station was two blocks off the town square, opposite the cheese shop and second hand store.

"I understand you're the quilt lady that's trying to save the old trees in the park." I nodded yes, as he continued. "I grew up in this town. Them trees been here longer'n me even an' that's long enuff. Guess there's some folks who'd like to see 'em cut down, or paved over, or what have you, but I've got a great-gran'baby coming soon an' I figures I'd like him to grow up'n see them trees too. I understand you ladies been doing all this work. So here, mebbe there's things you need." He rummaged in his pocket and stuck his hand out, passing me some rumpled bills.

"Thank you," I smiled. "But it's not necessary," I began, but he waved me off.

"Ain't necessary what yor doin' neither. It's just right." And with that he turned and loped out the door and across the park. I looked at the bills. There was eighty-seven dollars of pure gold and goodwill in my hand.

On another day, I saw Councilwoman Rita Appleton on the street. I smiled and nodded "Hello." But as soon as she saw me, she put her face down and raised her hands over her head, waving them as if she was swatting flies, and shook her head as she rushed past me. Obviously, she thought I was going to buttonhole her, give her my opinion, or solicit her vote. I wasn't going to, in fact. By her reaction I guessed that enough people had already been pestering her and she must have been fed up with the whole thing. I hoped if she was angry that at least she was angry at both sides, not just us. Maybe it would prove a mistake, but I felt that it wasn't appropriate to lobby the Council members themselves. They were the elected officials of the town. We had chosen a take-it-to-the-people, grassroots approach hoping that public opinion and common sense would win out. Time would tell.

The Wombats often met in my shop for strategy sessions after the close of business. One evening we were sitting around discussing our progress so far and trying to keep ourselves positive in the face of people's apathy, antipathy and antagonism, when a knock sounded on the door. We opened it to find a deliveryman with a box of take-away food for us. "Compliments of Ming Pak," we were told. It was the name of a popular local Vietnamese fast food chain, famous for its unusual cross-cultural concoctions. As we happily tucked into some delicious Sweet and Sour Seoul Ribs and Tex Mex Yakitori, it occurred to me that perhaps we had a lot of invisible and silently supportive allies out there after all. But it was a rollercoaster ride all summer.

The Downtown Merchants' Association met one evening in the church basement and reluctantly agreed that our plan was a good one but they didn't think we could pull it off. As a group they had a hopeless "there's nothing we can do" attitude. It was as if they were merely waiting for the axe to fall, waiting to be evicted by Little Al Junior. I was surprised that most of them continued to pay their rent to him. Under the circumstances, I would have withheld and saved my nickels. But everyone appeared to walk softly around Al as if he were a mean unpredictable dog. I thought he was just a big kid looking to get lucky. He scared me only in that he might indeed have luck on his side. And I doubted that he was as dumb as Jo would have me believe.

The only merchants who held out any hope were the few who still owned their own property. But we were the only hope we had, so that wasn't terribly encouraging. Their interest was purely self interest and commercial. They would be more than happy to participate in a renovation project, if we got it organized and funded. I guess that's people for you, but it was frustrating trying to get them to help themselves. For me, the final straw broke when two of the merchants approached me after the meeting and said they had decided to accept Al Junior's offer to buy their property. They had caught the "abandon ship" panic and nothing at the meeting had convinced them otherwise. I tried to accept their decision with good grace and understanding but inside I railed and wondered how much they had sold out for. I wondered if the price had gone up as the council meeting approached, but didn't have the nerve to ask.

Ruth, who was usually so negative, had been quiet during the meeting. Even though I didn't need any more rain on my parade I missed the negativity she usually shed and I suspected she was having second thoughts. Marlene told me that Ruth had some trouble with her husband and she might have wanted to sell her hair salon business to Al Junior just to run away from her problems. Maybe her husband was urging her to sell. I was angry with her for even considering selling out but if that were the case, I couldn't have blamed her. If things were different, I might have considered it too. Even so, I guess I wasn't too adept at disguising my irritability. She must have sensed it because she didn't stop to say goodnight at the end of the meeting, but slipped out the back door alone.

After the meeting Ivy and I walked back through the park together. We were half way across the park when I stopped and sat down on a bench in frustration.

"Why are we doing this?" I grumbled at her. Although she had been in Clareville longer than I had, her whole life, like mine, was now invested in a few hundred square feet of retail space on an old town square. "Are the Wombats the only ones who care about saving the downtown? Ivy, why don't we just give up?"

"Because we're doing what you know in your heart is right, love," she said in her soft Wexford accent. She sat down beside me and patted my arm reassuringly.

"But maybe the fight isn't worth it."

"I'm not sure we ever know for certain what a worthy purpose

in life is. You have to go with what is in your heart. Just because
people are apathetic, don't let that stop you. I've always believed
that things are only accomplished by people who try, not by the
people who care less or who are afraid. Believe me, love, I know."

She hesitated a moment before she spoke, softly and wistfully.
"You know, it was my first husband's dream to open a little restaurant. But Nigel never did anything about it. He was afraid people
would think he was crazy. He was always worried about what other
people would think. In the end he died without realizing his dream,
and so what did it matter? I've often thought since then, at least
it's better to die knowing that you tried."

"I had no idea," I said sympathetically. Such a shame, I thought.
And what a sad monument to her husband's life. Too bad he
hadn't been able to tap into some of Ivy's strength and courage.
Isn't that what marriage is all about—giving each other strength,
and using each other's courage.

"So you know what I did? I took the insurance money and opened
my restaurant. It should have been Nigel's." She looked away into
the distance, past the darkened storefront which bore her solitary
name, to that wistful place of if-only regrets. "Don't let go of your
dream without a fight," she said finally and patted my shoulder as
she stood up. "I think you are doing a great job, love."

"Thanks," I whispered weakly and stood up.

We parted to go our own ways home. I watched until I saw Ivy
safely leave the park and climb into her car, then I continued
across the common toward the gate nearest Grama's Quilt Shop.
I felt like Little Red Riding Hood walking through the woods to
grandma's house, and the story made me smile. It reminded me of
my own grandfather. When I was a little girl we lived in Chicago.
Grandpa used to sit me on his knee and tell me stories about a
little girl named Molly who had wonderful adventures in our
neighborhood but always seemed to end up being chased by "The
Big Bad Wolf of Bloor Street." The wolf had many disguises and
sometimes pretended to be her friend in order to get close to her,
manipulating her innocence and vulnerability. Yet no matter how

tricky the wolf was or how fast he chased her, she always managed to race home just in time to slam the door in his face. I was enthralled, terrified and then exhilarated at her inevitable last-minute triumphs. I knew even at the time that he meant for me to see myself as Molly, the courageous and resourceful heroine who could see through all the wolf's deceptions, and of course I did.

Now what would make me think of that after all these years, I puzzled. What had he been telling me in those homespun fairy tales?

I came to a stop on the footpath just before the gate. Above me, the shadowy tops of massive dark trees swished softly in the night breeze. There were circles of yellow illumination from the streetlights outside the park, while I was engulfed in profound shadows made stark by the full white moon against a cloudless black sky. I was in the deep forest of the wolf. In the distance, car sounds and street noises drifted in vaguely, muffled by the bushes and trees. Flashes from far away sheets of heat lightning momentarily lit the horizon followed by remote rumbling grumbles. I stepped off the walkway and moved over to the nearest oak tree. On an impulse I sat down and leaned against it. Its dry old bark was scratchy through my cotton shirt. All the birds and animals were asleep. Only the rustling trees and I were awake in all the world.

"I'm just a little girl fighting clever wolves in order to stay alive," I said aloud to the dark woods. The looming tree seemed to answer with an encompassing warmth. "I'm here," it seemed to say.

I almost forgot about you, I thought to the tree.

Yes, here is this small forest, I remarked to myself, imbedded in an urban sea of bricks and mortar. We have isolated it from its kind, from its mother forest of this great land, yet here it stands defending us, breathing free oxygen into our air and providing green nurture to us all. Surely we must now be responsibile for it. What are we doing tearing down these ancient loyal guardians, I thought indignantly.

I felt very small and humble in the tree's embrace.

This isn't just about me and my little shop of troubles, I realized, suddenly uncomfortable with my own self-seeking interests. I had been angry because I was thwarted in my attempts to make everyone see things my way. It might be about saving the downtown core of this community and its failing economy, but it was more than that, I thought as I saw our little village in my mind's eye. It was about every small town. If we keep demolishing each one soon there will be no small towns left. There will be no Small Town America to tell stories about, to be the birthplace of individuals, and values. The hue and cry about the lack of family values in society would have no remembered roots in any of us except from a dry and impersonal historical perspective. They would be like missing pages in a book. Sometimes when we move on, we leave our valuables behind. Soon there'll be no one left who remembers what small town America was all about. No one will remember the "before" times.

The issue that was absorbing the town was also about the park itself. It was not enough to want to keep the park and trees so that I could enjoy them. It was about the trees themselves and what they symbolized. It was about the past, and about our relationship to the environment, and our future in it. The problem was that we called this greenspace an "it," as if the woods and the larger world were something outside ourselves—that we were not imbedded in it. This little forest was a living entity, like a relative or a member of our community. It was a "thou" that we should be honoring. We are all creations, all cousins of a common growing root. I am the quilter, but I do not own the creativity, any more than the seed owns the tree that comes from it. I am temporarily the caretaker of the quilt. If I treasure it, my creation will pass on to other hands. We have to learn to live in the world, not pull it apart at the seams. We're meant to live compatibly with the earth, in harmony.

Ivy, there is a worthy purpose, I decided with satisfaction as I stood up at last. A peacefulness and calm determination had filled my heart.

"Thank you, friend tree, for the reminder." As I spoke I suddenly remembered our son Robbie when he was a little boy learning to talk, and I smiled. He spoke to everything. He would cheerfully say, "Hello table," "Hello grass," "Bye Bye beach," as if everything were alive and he merely a polite and curious human moving through the wondrous world around him. It was his innocence and unwitting wisdom at the same time that charmed me. He never lost his curiosity and respect for life, and ended up studying oceanography, the science of the ocean, the mother waters from which all life on the planet springs.

I patted the rough bark affectionately and stepped back on the pathway which led home. For once the wolf was not chasing me. A weather front moved in behind me from the south and a cool breeze swayed the branches, scooting me along the path. As I passed through the stone arch of the western gate of the park, the gate of the raven and the bear, the gate of twilight and introspection, overhead the shooshing leaves seemed to say in farewell, se-e-e you, se-e-e you around.

THE NEXT DAY RUTH CALLED and asked if I would meet her for lunch. I accepted, reluctantly, because I suspected she was about to give me bad news. I was surprised when she picked me up and drove to a restaurant on the edge of town. (I had automatically assumed we would go to Ivy's.) Maybe she didn't want Ivy to overhear our conversation, I decided. On the way we kept up a steady but light conversation about general happenings in the world. Running a hair salon gave Ruth an irreverent inside perspective on local gossip. We weren't talking about the town square, and she was amusing company.

The restaurant she chose was a strange concoction called The Red Mill Station. It was a converted house with a huge old water wheel on one side, hence the "mill," but with no stream in sight, and a Pullman railway car attached to the other, hence "station". Everything was painted bright red. Inside was a rabbit warren of small rooms connected to a central dining room which contained an elaborate buffet and salad bar. We were seated and offered drinks. When the waiter disappeared, Ruth poked around in her purse and finally pulled out a coupon with torn edges. As she held it up I noticed a large bluish mark on her forearm.

"That's a bad bruise you have there," I commented.

"Oh, it's nothing." She shrugged. "I dropped a gallon jug of shampoo on myself." She quickly pulled down the sleeve of her sweater to cover the mark. "Bill's always telling me what a klutz I am."

"Oh," I said and let it pass.

"It's a buy-one-get-one-free," she said sheepishly as she slipped the coupon under the edge of her placemat and patted it into place.

"That's okay," I reassured her. "Every little bit helps."

"Isn't that the truth," she sighed. "Bill doesn't like this place." She fiddled with the silverware and mostly kept her eyes down as we talked, except when she would look up at me quickly and then lower her face again, almost shyly. It was as if she were trying to be serious and formal when underneath she felt tense and nervous. It wasn't like Ruth at all. I always found her to be direct and down-to-earth. I kept waiting for the shoe to drop but there seems to be a peculiar order to these things and I had to hold my patience until the right time. She had obviously brought me here to tell me something. The ball was in Ruth's court. We made our way to the buffet, filled plates with chicken and shrimp and potato salad and made mundane comments about the various dishes and pretty display, then returned to our table and began to eat. She finally spoke her mind.

"You know I've been thinking of selling to Al Junior."

"Un-huh," I said without emotion.

Then, between forkfuls of food, she told me all the economic reasons. It sounded as though she had memorized Al's report. She didn't owe me an explanation. Besides I'd heard it all before. She was blowing smoke. I suspected that wasn't the real reason so I just kept quiet.

"It's not that I *want* to, you understand," she finally explained with emphasis. "It's just that I may have to leave town."

Have to, she said. That was it. "Why?" I asked. "Don't you like it here?"

"Yes. Yes, I do." She munched a leaf of lettuce. "I like it here a lot, but I'm . . . thinking of leaving Bill." She said it so matter-of-factly that she had apparently been thinking about it a great deal. Enough for it to be a familiar thought even if she'd never voiced it out loud before. She had planned this lunch in order to tell me and when she did, the tension seemed to gush out of her as if she were relieved that she had finally stepped off a cliff.

"Oh," I said. "I'm sorry," and waited. I'd done a lot of listening. I sensed that she had more to say.

"I figured you'd understand these things," she mumbled into her plate. "You've probably heard it all before—" she trailed off.

"That's okay," I reassured her. Everyone's pain is unique and personal and deserves the space to be heard.

Several moments passed while Ruth took a sip of water and toyed with her chicken. "Bill can be, well, you know... *difficult*... to live with," she said with a meaningful look. With that she began to unburden herself, telling me the story of her increasingly unhappy marriage. She spoke in a remarkably calm and detached manner, as if she were discussing hair color or the latest makeup tips. Being in a public place gave her the strength not to break down emotionally.

"Oh Ruth, I'm so sorry," I said as my heart fell. I reached across the table and held her hand. I felt sick imagining what she had been going through. I understood from her oblique comments and inferences that there was physical abuse involved, and I immediately regretted my hard feelings toward her. Every pulse of anger I felt toward her melted away.

Ruth simply looked up at me, smiled and shrugged as if that was just her lot in life.

"How long?"

"Oh, it usually doesn't last long. Probably only a few minutes I suppose," she answered, staring off into space as if she were trying to focus a picture accurately.

"No. I mean has this been going on for a long time?"

"Oh, yes," she sighed and casually spooned up some potato salad. "Ever since we were married."

I was staggered. They had been married twenty-eight years.

"But it's not all the time," she explained quickly. "Just sometimes. Every once in a while when things get to him, you know, he lashes out."

"Oh, Ruth. That's terrible. You two can get help, you know."

She laughed cynically. "Bill says it's my fault. It's my fault when he gets fired from a job and when the kids got into trouble it was my fault for not controlling them. He says I'm the one with the problem."

"They all do," I said angrily. I'd dealt with this before. But Ruth wasn't a client of mine, she had become a friend. I didn't have to remain professionally detached. That was the problem with being a therapist. You go into it because you care about people and want to help. Then you spend years training yourself to be detached and not to become personally involved. Thank God I didn't have to do that any more. I was sick of not feeling, of not holding someone close when they were in pain. I guessed that she had recently been going through a particularly bad time. I kicked myself for not noticing before.

"And he's really not that bad. People like Bill. You know most of the time, we get along really fine. It's just, well . . ."

"Ruth. Ruth. Ruth," I shook my head. I should have known better. I had criticized him and she then felt she had to defend him. It never ceases to amaze me that women are so unbelievably loyal. In spite of everything she could defend him. She probably even truly loved him. Maybe she couldn't believe that the man she loved could be so awful. It was love and denial at the same time. How would Mrs. Jekyll and Hyde have felt?

Ruth figured the only answer was to run away where Bill

couldn't find her. I think it was a salvation fantasy which even she knew wasn't the solution.

We finished coffee and headed back to work. The silence in the car underlined that there was little else to say. When she dropped me at my shop I hugged her tightly. "Anything I can do—" I assured her.

"Thanks," she said, ". . . for listening."

For two days afterward I shook my head in disbelief at Ruth's revelations. People are always more than we think they are, I reminded myself. There are often terrible and deep secrets that lay buried inside people, even those who we think are open and superficially happy. The more I thought about Ruth's troubles, the angrier I became. It made me appreciate how lucky I was that Jack had been such a good partner. Does anyone get that lucky twice in life, I wondered. Not likely. I thought about Daniel and speculated on what had prompted his divorce, what was buried under his smiling surface. Suddenly, his secretiveness made me uneasy and I decided that I couldn't go out with him. I called him on Thursday to cancel.

"What's the matter?" he asked with concern. "Did I say something wrong?"

"No," I said firmly. "I just can't get involved with anyone right now." Where had I heard that recently? But at least it was true. I was already too busy to deal with a new relationship. Even though I was attracted to Daniel, it was an excuse to avoid letting a man get close to me.

"Aggie, it's only dinner!" he cajoled with a soft laugh.

He wasn't taking me seriously. That made me mad. "No. I just... can't," I said with finality.

He exhaled loudly into the telephone. "Whatever you say," he said with obvious annoyance.

"Fine. Bye." I hung up quickly. How dare he be angry because I wouldn't go out with him. I was so agitated that I paced up and down the shop for several minutes until I cooled down.

"And *don't* you say a word!" I pointed my finger threateningly at Grama. She didn't, but she shook her head sadly while I paced. Apparently she thought I was being irrational, and maybe it was true. But I already had too many commitments. It didn't need any more complications.

THE NEXT WOMBATS MEETING was at my shop that same evening. Everyone was sitting around the cutting table, waiting for Marlene who was a few minutes late. I was in the back room making coffee and tea and I heard them animatedly whispering about something and laughing. When I emerged carrying a large tray, Ruth called out cheerfully, "So what's this about you and Fireman Dan?" Of all people it would have to be Ruth to hear gossip, working in her beauty salon.

"What do you mean?" I stalled.

"Well, I hear he's been asking around town about you."

"Oh, I can't imagine why," I replied casually. "He's been in the shop once or twice I believe." I shrugged and busied myself with the mugs. I didn't know if she knew about our dinner date, or my cancelling it.

"He had her in stitches one day in the shop," Joyce interjected helpfully. I gave her a hard look to shut her up.

"So, don't act like you're not interested, girl," Jo scolded playfully. "He's a sweetheart, and eligible."

"He certainly seems interested in you," Ruth carried on.

"Mom. How come you never said anything?" Susan accused playfully. She turned to Millie. "We ran into him at the baseball game. He seemed really nice but Mom played it so cool." Millie nodded and shrugged.

"It's really nothing," I said defensively.

"Aggie's got a boyfriend!" Ivy said and they all started to chant like schoolgirls in a playground.

Fortunately at that moment Marlene waltzed through the door. Thank goodness, everyone's attention turned to Marlene. We all watched in amused curiosity as she bounced and "flew" her briefcase around the room before landing it in the middle of the table.

"Guess what I've got," she chuckled and patted the case. "Ta da!" she opened it with a flourish. "As if by magic!" She pulled out a worn yellow file folder.

"Armbruster's papers!" cried Viola when she recognized her old records.

"How did you get them?"

"Where—"

"When—"

We yelled, and hugged her.

"Easy," she replied with feigned nonchalance. "I was working late tonight, killing time doing some paperwork while waiting for the meeting, and it occurred to me that maybe Al Junior hadn't burned the papers. If he hadn't, where would he have put them? On a long shot I thought maybe, just maybe, he put them in the office safe. What he doesn't realize, and nobody else in our real estate office does either, is that I know the combination. How I got the combination is another story," she said with a wink. "When Little Al took over as manager of the office, he never bothered to change the combination. I've found it a useful thing to know and not have anyone know that I know, if you see what I mean. And there they were," she finished.

"How could he be so careless, to keep them right there in the safe?" I exclaimed.

It's never a good idea to underestimate your enemy but it looked as if this time, old age and cunning had beat out youth and inexperience! It was a triumph and we needed one.

Marlene turned to Millie. "Sorry, Mil."

Millie looked disgusted. She flicked her lighter angrily and lit up a cigarette, not even bothering to take it outside even though she knew I had a No Smoking policy and she always observed it without my having to say anything. "I'll kill him," she spat. "I don't care what else he does in life but I didn't raise him to be a thief."

Ivy patted her arm. "Go easy, love. He's just a boy. He probably thought it wouldn't hurt anyone. He didn't destroy the documents so maybe he planned to return them."

"No excuse," Millie replied.

"Well, just don't act too quickly, Millie. I need time to work on the Preservation Order," Marlene warned. "There's a good possibility that he won't miss the papers right away. It's going to take some real pushing to get this through the bureaucratic jungle in time for the Council meeting. In the meantime we'll have to get a temporary injunction to stop him from tearing the building down."

"He's going to know you broke into the safe," Ivy observed. "He might fire you."

"Sometimes I wish he would. Then I could spend more time painting. But he can't fire me without admitting he stole the papers in the first place," Marlene pointed out. "I don't think he wants his name in the paper that way, do you?"

"Good point," Ivy agreed.

"The worst that can happen is that he changes the combination lock. It doesn't matter now anyway. There hasn't been anything really dishy in there since he's been Manager anyway," Marlene shrugged.

"No pictures of town Councillors in compromising positions we could use as blackmail?" Ruth suggested hopefully.

"I should hope not!" Millie shot across the table.

"Sorry, Mrs. Mayor," Ruth smiled in mock sheepish apology.

This was just what we needed. It would take some fast footwork but with the Armbruster papers we could get a preservation order and with that maybe we could stop Al Junior and the big city boys. Or at least divert the steamroller. It was beginning to feel like an intense Monopoly game, and we just put a big fat hotel on Park Place.

It was an exciting meeting after that. I was relieved that everyone seemed to have forgotten about Daniel and me. We were all laughing and talking and plotting when Jennifer came slamming in the front door.

"What's the matter, honey?" I called out to her.

As she stepped into the circle of light, she exclaimed, "I've been sleeping with the enemy!" Seeing my raised eyebrows she hastened to add, "Figuratively speaking, of course."

"I can't believe he would do this to me!" she railed.

"Who? Did what?" I asked in concern. Everyone's attention was riveted on her.

"Deceived me!"

"Who are you talking about?"

"Al Junior, alias 'AJ', the guy I had dinner with. All along he tells me his name is AJ, says 'my friends call me AJ'. I didn't know it was Little Al Junior! Your son!" She pointed a finger at Millie. "He deceived me. Here we are having this nice dinner at Santiago's. We're talking, you know, getting acquainted. I tell him about being fired from the bank and Jim, and everything. Finally he tells me about his business stuff here in town, his plan to build a great big mall downtown. His plan! Big shot! That's when I realized he was the enemy!"

"So what did you do?" Ivy asked.

"Well, I did the only thing I could do," she said imperiously. "I stood up and walked out."

We all laughed, except Jennifer, who was obviously deadly serious and mad.

"I would have waited until after dessert, myself. They have fabulous tiramisu there," chuckled Jo.

"Whoa . . . Calm down, girl," I soothed Jennifer. "Maybe he didn't know who you were," I suggested helpfully.

"Yeah. Like nobody in town knows you, the quilt shop lady, or that I'm your daughter!"

"He met you, remember, that first day you came to town. Did you tell him then who you were related to?" Ivy asked.

"No."

"And besides, why didn't you know who he was, since *you* know *his* mother," Millie pointed out sarcastically.

"Good point," I agreed. "Well, it's nice to know he prefers to be called AJ," I commented to Millie. She nodded. It was a small point of interest to share.

At that Jennifer grew huffy, since she wasn't receiving enough sympathy.

"Oh, cool it, Jen," ordered Susan finally. "It's no big deal."

"No big deal? Well, if I hadn't figured out who he was—"

"Yeah, like that was real difficult since he came right out and told you," Susan laughed.

"He might have pumped me for information about the Wombats and our plans," she asserted, ignoring her sister's interruption.

"Our plans are all pretty public," I said.

"Besides he's not smart enough to be that deceptive," Jo added.

I guess we were all keyed up, and Millie had reached her high water mark. She turned and glared hard at Jo. Through clenched teeth her foot long a's stretched into yards as she said, "He was sma-a-at enough to buy up ha-a-alf the property on the town squa-a-a-ah, and he was sma-a-at enough to attract the attention of a la-a-a-ahg development company! What do you want him to do, *brain surgery?*"

An embarrassed silence fell over the room.

"Maybe we should take a recess here," I suggested. "We're all getting tense as the Council meeting gets closer. Why don't we take a coffeebreak. Let me get you a fresh cup, Mil."

As we stood up to stretch, I saw Jo put her hand on Millie's arm and say softly, "Sorry." Millie readily dipped her head with a nod of forgiveness, and a touch of sadness I thought. They were tough times for her. She had her own opinions and work to do on the Wombats' behalf. She also had to live with a son whose business project she opposed and a husband who was notorious for sitting on fences. It probably said something positive about AJ that he still lived at home. Their relationship must normally have been a pretty good one. We were lucky Millie was working with us. What inner turmoil she must be facing, I thought sympathetically. Love and loyalty made her defend her son, integrity and conscience made her oppose him. Apparently her husband and son had their own trouble getting along right now, too. She must have felt like the ham in a ham sandwich.

Throughout the evening, Millie drank several cups of coffee and I noticed that she seemed thinner than usual. I wondered if she was eating enough, or just worrying the weight off. And she smoked too much. Every few minutes stood up and went to the door to light up a cigarette, blowing the smoke outside. My mother died a miserable death from lung cancer and I hated to see some-one else killing herself like that. I was worried about Jo, too. She looked tired and I wondered if she wasn't feeling well. She hadn't said anything about her doctor's visit, but since she kept up her usual hectic pace, I assumed everything was all right. They were stressful times all around as we counted down the days to the next Council meeting.

At the end of the meeting, Ruth held back and was the last to leave. Jennifer and Susan were clearing up the coffee things as I stood at the door bidding everyone goodnight. Ruth leaned close to me and said, "I'm sorry if I embarrassed you. Daniel is really a nice guy. Why don't you give him a try?"

How could Ruth, after everything she'd gone through, be so optimistic as to encourage me to get involved with anyone.

I looked at the dozen large STOP posters which filled the front windows of my shop.

"We'll see," I replied non-commitally. Maybe I had been too rash in canceling dinner, but it was too late, I told myself. I wasn't about to call him, and besides, even if I did he would probably think I was nuts.

I waved goodbye to Ruth as she drove away. "I'll lock up," I called to the girls. "Turn off the lights and I'll see you upstairs." I took out my keys. Just as I started to close the door behind me from the outside, Jennifer poked her head around the backroom door and asked, "Mom, when are you going to replace that stupid chain?"

I unhooked the open padlock from the chain where I usually left it hanging during the day, and hefted it in my hand. "I don't know," I said quietly, looking down at the weight on my palm. "I guess I've gotten used to it now."

Jen didn't hear me. She hadn't really expected or waited for an answer. I slipped the lock through the chain and snapped it shut, giving it one last reassuring yank before turning toward the stairs and home.

LATER THAT EVENING after the girls had gone to bed, I returned to the shop by the inner staircase and finished hand sewing my last quilt block with faithful Hobbes lying at my elbow. Sitting at the cutting table had become a calming ritual I looked forward to every evening. As I stitched I recalled the meeting and thought about Millie again. I realized that there was a woman whose vote on the issue could reasonably go either way, and rightfully so. How did she decide where her sentiments and loyalty lay?

My own vested interests were all one way. AJ's were slanted another way. The merchants' were somewhere in between. The members of Council had their own goals for their town. And although perhaps not directly involved, the townspeople had their opinions too. Everyone had their own viewpoint. So who was right, I puzzled. How could Council possibly weigh the conflicting interests and decide who would be winners and who would be losers? It was so complicated, so tangled up. I wanted things to be simple. I moved to Clareville to simplify my life. Yet here I am in the thick of things again. I wanted there to be one ultimate truth, only one shade of gray, one righteous side. It bothered me. We were like the seven blind men trying to describe an elephant by feeling just one part of it. Each one perceived it to be something different—a wall, a hose, a rope, a tree trunk. But it was still an elephant.

When I realized that, something clicked into place, and I understood that in fact everyone was right, everyone did have a righteous perspective. Suddenly, I was able to see AJ in my mind's eye objectively. I pictured AJ from his mother's point of view as a young businessman proudly telling an enthralled young lady on a first date about his wonderful plan for the town. And when I saw him as such, as if he were my own son, I forgave him.

After that, I envisioned the merchants as hardworking businesspeople, worried about their future and their families, trying to do the best they could with their resources, and I forgave them, also. And then I tried to stretch my mind around all the townspeople, who had their own world of troubles and their own perspectives, and I accepted in my heart that they too were okay. Sometimes we get caught up in our judgements of other people, and sometimes we have to suspend those judgements in order to see clearly, I thought.

It made me feel somewhat wistful, but a whole lot more peaceful to let go of my anger and hard feelings. Grama came to mind then. It seemed like a long time since I'd heard from her; I hadn't had the time to call her up. I waited to hear her say something wise about my "aha" realization but she didn't. She just smiled and nodded. That was all. That was enough.

It was compassion that I had felt. That's what Grama would have said.

Then I remembered seeing a quilt block years ago, called *Tangled Briars*. I always recognized it because I often confused it with the *Delectable Mountains* block. They have similar pieces and are actually variations of a commonly rooted design comprised of squares and right-angled triangles. In *Delectable Mountains*, the spokey "mountain" triangles all line up one way, in an orderly row, like a chain of mountains should. It could represent a sacred place of wisdom where the upward struggle leads you closer to heaven. In *Tangled Briars*, the same pieces alternate up-down and in-out like a burr or the confused and sticky mess of vegetation they may represent. As Peter Rabbit found out, it's hard to climb through the briar patch without leaving a tell-tale piece of fur behind.

That night I decided that *Tangled Briars* would be my next quilt block because out of confusion I could take the same basic pieces and reorganize them into *Delectable Mountains*. Out of a negative and irritating emotional burr, could come the mountain of serenity and grace. Wasn't that the answer to the duality and mystery of life? Out of challenge and chaos, with effort, comes order. Out of confusion, anger and frustration, with compassion, come peace and wisdom. Our job is to clear our vision, to see with the eyes of love and understanding both the positive and the negative. To enfold all opposites into our being. That was the end of the roller-coaster cycle of struggle and ecstasy.

If I believed in myself I could be merciful with everyone else. By exercising compassion for the entire community, I realized that I had gained the right to be there. Compassion for the world had taken me past the conflict of reconciling opposites. Manhood is about distinctions and separation. Womanhood is about embracing and enfolding. I thought of the forest on the mountainside and the fluid water of the ocean that symbolizes our deepest consciousness, and of how when we lock away parts of our nature or destroy nature itself we cut off a vital portion of our reality. We deny the complete realm of human existence.

I took a deep breath. Then I took two more and let go of my judgements.

SEVEN

Summer Storms

THE CORN WAS HIGH IN AUGUST. The ground was green and fertile, bearing abundant squashes and melons and peaches. The sky was heavy and damp, and the town slept like Brigadoon. Rain brought no relief.

As I drove by the fields around Clareville one day I remembered the summer visits to grandmother's farm I made as a child. Years later, when I saw Ray Kinsella in *Field of Dreams*, I was reminded of the hot afternoons when I would walk through Grandmother's corn fields with the tall green stalks brushing against my shoulders. I would imagine that I, too, heard voices in the rustling. Sometimes it used to scare me silly. I was afraid I would get lost. It's easy to feel disoriented in the high corn. Ten feet into the field might as well have been a hundred. The crowding green obliterates your sense of direction—you lose your perspective, your vision of distant horizons, in the immediacy of in-your-face foliage.

I rarely ventured into the cornfield alone because I became confused. One day, my cousin, Bob, and I were playing tag, crashing around in the obscuring greenery when I suddenly realized I had lost his voice and the noise of his moving through the corn stalks. He had sneaked away. He was trying to scare me, as boys will do—and it worked. I panicked. I ran in every direction. I yelled. I jumped futilely toward the blue dome sky for bearings. I cursed Bob. The sun was high and hot overhead. A buzzing of insects surrounded me, harassing me. My heart pounded in my ears. I held my hands over my eyes to close out the confusion and panic.

Then in the tumult it suddenly came to me. In the sightless dark I heard grandmother's quiet voice. "Don't be scared," she said. "Think."

"Corn is planted in straight rows, silly," I said to myself as I opened my eyes again. "Follow the row to the edge of the field."

The panic left me. I didn't know where I was, or where the row would lead me, but at least I knew how to get home. When I emerged I was dusty, tired and a half mile from home. I could see grandmother standing on the porch waiting. Bob was sitting dejected on the step, in trouble for having abandoned me. I didn't have to be angry anymore. Grandmother would bawl him out for both of us.

In the end, I had walked the long way through the field, but I could finally see where I was. I learned that staying on a straight path, staying true to that path, would ultimately lead me somewhere familiar.

CORN TURNED UP AGAIN when Millie and Al held a barbeque and corn roast. Fortunately AJ wasn't going to be there, and I was relieved. I had already had an unplesant encounter with AJ the week before when one morning I received a curious telephone call from him. He offered to buy my property. He was in a hurry, he said, and had an offer ready to fax over to me. (As if a quilt shop would have a fax machine, I laughed to myself.) It sounded too much like a high pressure sales tactic. Ironically, I had wondered when he would get around to me, as he had with all the other merchant-owners. He made his offer over the telephone, and it was a sizable one. He must have heard about the merchant association and the campaigning we were doing. Perhaps he was concerned that the opposition to his proposal was growing stronger, and by silencing me, there would be less to contend with. I was perversely complimented that he thought I was influential. In another place and time, his call would have upset me. It might even have tempted me. I would have been indignant and angry, or even intimidated into the temptation of selling out. But by then I was just quietly amused, and just said "no," which seemed to irritate him severely. He hung up with a veiled threat that he wasn't prepared to repeat his offer and that I might be sorry some day. Maybe he's been too used to getting his own way lately, I thought. Yes, he's just a spoiled pup, I decided as I hung up the telephone. No fault of Millie's. Parents can only do so much. At some point in everyone's life they begin to make their own decisions and are responsibile for their own actions. If AJ was a bully in business, it was his own responsibility. And he would own the consequences too.

Mille's barbecue was supposed to be a casual family get-together with friends, but she had arranged to invite the influential people that Al suggested might be interested in privately financing the downtown redevelopment. It was going to be an opportunity to informally button-hole them and gauge their interest. Marlene and I were invited as pitchmen. We were also the only single females in the group and it dawned on me that we had better tread lightly. The men in these powerful couples might have had control of the money, but it was clear that the women wouldn't let them spend it on a widow and a divorcee.

I made this observation to Marlene on the drive over to Al and Millie's. Marlene had picked me up in her Lincoln Continental. She said it would be more impressive than my minivan. I said I didn't think anyone would notice what we were driving.

"They're more likely to notice what we're *wearing*," I commented pointedly. Marlene was wearing shorts and a low-cut halter top in a flamboyant print of neon bananas and strawberries. Against her dark brown skin, the black background disappeared and made it look as though she was wearing nothing but fruity decals.

"It's just a barbeque," she replied, unconcerned.

"Yeah, but there's going to be more than steaks sizzling . . ." I intimated.

She looked at me and followed my eyes down to her chest. Her cleavage was ample and very visible. "Oh, oh," she said, suddenly realizing her misjudgement. "Oh dear. Well, here's what we'll do.

You drive." She pulled the car over abruptly, stopped and jumped into the backseat. I slid over. Her backseat, I noticed, was full of clothes. I thought she was taking them to the cleaners. "I always keep a change of clothing in the car," she explained as she began to rummage. "For emergencies." She laughed.

"Emergencies? You could *live* in your car," I joked.

"Girlfriend, there was a time when I thought I'd have to."

I watched her in the rearview mirror as I put the car into gear and pulled back onto the road. There was everything from an expensive tailored suit to a bright tribal caftan, even a strapless fuschia number which could have lit up a dance floor all on its own. I wondered what kind of emergencies Marlene found herself in. I decided then and there that with Marlene's vitality and sense of color she was a natural to join a quilting class.

"How's this?" she asked holding up a nondescript linen suit.

I peered into the mirror and shook my head. "Think country club brunch, not hallelujah picnic," I suggested. She laughed.

"That's it," I agreed as she finally held up a casual but elegant saffron-colored silk pantsuit. She shucked out of her clothes and began redressing.

"You know, I've been wanting to ask you what made you go into real estate in the first place," I said by way of making conversation.

"Money," she replied. "Years ago when my husband left me... no offence, but he was white, and he was a bum—"

"None taken."

"After that I had to work. I have two boys to raise. So I looked around for a job that would pay me more the harder I worked. Real estate was it. I like straight commissions. The more I hustle my buns, the more money I make. Besides, when I looked around at the guys in the business, making a go of it and supporting their families, I figured I could too."

"Well, you've certainly made a success of it," I complimented her.

"Yeah, I found out that I'm good at it," she replied, as she zipped and buttoned up. Even a luxury car didn't provide much room to change clothes. Not that I would know. "That's the problem."

"Problem? Why is it a problem being good at something?"

"Because I'd rather be slapping paint onto canvas."

"You paint?" I asked in surprise. "Good for you!"

"Yeah. Portraits mostly. That's what I'd do if I won the lottery. There's the house," she said, pointing down the block. We had turned onto Millie's street and our conversation was interrupted as we turned our attention to the more pressing matters at hand.

IN THE END THE BARBEQUE was a success. It was a fun afternoon with children over-running the lawn, splashing in the pool and trying to play tennis on the red clay court. "Uncle Al" played the part of host to perfection. He was jovial, gregarious and entertaining. Wearing a well-stained butcher's apron that read "Kiss the Cook," he obviously loved manning the flames. Millie adroitly manouevered us into conversations with everyone. I made sure I talked with every one of the wives. I thought it was important to gain their support for the redevelopment project. I felt more optimistic about the possiblity that some of these influential people would be prepared to join a consortium of private investors to finance the renovations we were proposing. Thanks to t-bones and cobs of corn, the doors were at least open.

At one point early in the afternoon an elderly man in an ex-pensive blue silk suit approached me and introduced himself and his diminutive wife. "So honored to meet you," he said, shaking my hand enthusiastically. I was surprised that my notoriety was so widespread. He turned to his wife, gesturing toward me. "Wife of first friend in Clareville," he explained. "One time, only friend," he said as he turned to me again, with a big grin. I was embar-rassed that I didn't know who he was but the man just smiled kindly and told me how he came to meet Jack, a long time ago.

It was 1964. Jack was a fifteen year old student at Dalton Rimple High School. The man and his family had recently moved to town, into a poor shanty on bottom land across the Clare River. They opened a small restaurant and struggled to stay in business. There was tremendous animosity toward him and his family. He described how his five children were often chased home by taunting, stone-throwing schoolmates. I nodded with understanding as I thought about how sometimes a small town can be an unwelcoming closed community when you are a newcomer, especially if you are different in any sort of way.

That was also the year of Hurricane Hazel, and the terrible storm flooded the riverbanks and all the low-lying farmland around Clareville. Volunteer brigades went out hour-after-hour to help sandbag houses and rescue people trapped by the rising water. They managed to save everyone and every house, except my storyteller's. He saw the rescue parties across the river but the whole town just seemed to ignore their cries for help. Until finally one lone rowboat set off across the slow-moving muddy water. There was only one person in the boat, a thin, drenched young man who struggled to keep the oars cutting through the water. The stranded man and his family watched anxiously from one side of the river as the townsfolk watched from the other. It took several minutes to make the crossing and by the time the rowboat reached the other side a small armada of boats had set off following his lead. When the young man arrived, exhausted and smiling broadly, he reached out for the woman's hand and said, "Anyone for take-away?"

And that was Jack.

Jack never told me the story himself, but it didn't surprise me. It was nice to know that there were still people in town who remembered Jack fondly. He always used to say that he was "just a small town boy". In fact, he was the town, and the town was in him wherever he went. It was a community that ultimately extended its hand in compassion and warmth, and even friendship, in a way that only small towns can.

"Looks like you really made an impression there," Marlene remarked as the man and his wife walked away to join the other

guests. He left me with his business card and an invitation to call
him next week. "Wouldn't that be great if we could get Ming Pak's
Oriental Express franchise to head up our financing proposal?"

"DO YOU MIND IF WE STOP at my house on the way back?" Marlene
asked as we drove back toward downtown at twilight. "I like to
drop in when the boys aren't expecting me. In case they snuck
some girls in."

"Not at all," I replied. I was feeling mellow and peaceful after
the wine and sunshine.

A couple of minutes later she pulled up to a modest brick
house. "I'm putting my money into education funds for my boys,"
she explained, unnecessarily. She opened the front door and gestured me inside. At a quick glance, I saw that the interior was
decorated with modern and comfortable furniture. It had the familiar disarray and lived-in look of a home with teenagers. I was
glad she didn't feel it necessary to apologize for the clutter. From
upstairs came booming music and from downstairs the squeaks
and roar of a basketball game on television.

"Ben! Chris!" Marlene called out in a loud voice. "Come here!"

Moments later two lanky boys shuffled into the room. They
were all baggy t-shirt, big feet and shyness. Marlene made introductions all around and the boys shook hands politely.

"Watcha been doin'?" Marlene asked them accusingly with a
stern look but a subtle twinkle in her eye.

"Nothin'!" came the defensive chorused reply.

"Good. Keep at it," she ordered and broke into a grin. "Now
git." She shooed them away again, saying, "There's Rocky Road in
the freezer."

"Thanks, Mom," they smiled and made for the kitchen. The
younger boy passed by his Mom and gave her a little kiss in passing.

"Nice boys," I complimented her. She was obviously proud
enough to burst.

"Most of the time." She shrugged. "Say, you're an artistic soul. Would you like to see some of my paintings?"

"Of course I would," I said eagerly.

Marlene led me to the family room where over the fireplace hung a large portrait of Martin Luther King Jr., looking out into the distance smiling. His hand was on the head of a little girl in pig-tails tied with colorful ribbons. King looked young and vital, and every inch the visionary.

"You did this?" I exclaimed. "It's remarkable! You are a talented artist! Marlene, this is spectacular!" I went to admire the painting up close. "Is this you?" I asked about the little girl.

"Why, yes," she replied, pleased and surprised at my intuition. "I met him. Once. When I was a little girl. He gave a sermon at our church. My parents spoke to him afterward. I knew he was a famous man and I was in awe of him, but he was so kind to me. He put his hand on my head, just like that." She paused and looked lovingly at the painting and into her memories. "I felt like I'd been blessed by the Pope. He was the closest thing we had to God."

After that she took me to her office. She had converted one of the bedrooms into space for her real estate work but in one crowded corner was an easel and a chaos of painting materials. There was a stack of canvases, some finished, some works in progress. Around the house, she showed me several other portraits she had done, mostly from memory of people she knew and loved. I remembered Picasso had once said that painting was just another way of keeping a diary, and that was what Marlene had done, kept a record of these people for her family to treasure and pass on.

"Marlene, you are a talented painter. You should do more of this," I told her. "Why don't you do this professionally?"

"Because I've got bills to pay," she replied candidly.

In the end we spent over two hours talking about painting and creativity and the sacrifices people have to make in life, the priorities of existence and responsibility which too often take precedence over the joyful things we could do, and need to do, for our souls. She asked me about giving up my own professional career to "go barefoot and native" as she called it. I told her about a carved wooden plaque I remembered seeing at a girlfriend's house when I was fifteen. Her parents had escaped from Germany just before the war broke out. The sign said: We get too soon old, and too late smart.

ON THE FOLLOWING MONDAY, I was drinking my usual morning coffee when the phone rang. It jarred me. No one usually called that early. It was Millie and her voice sounded awful.

"What's wrong?" I asked immediately.

"Aggie." I heard her take a long drag on a cigarette. "Jo's son, Jeremy, called. There was a car accident. Jo ran off the road. She's dead, Aggie."

Jo dead! I couldn't believe it. I was stunned. I had seen her just a few days earlier.

"Oh no," I kept repeating as Millie filled in the details.

I knew that Jo had left on Friday to drive to Cleveland. There was a national convention for JoBelle Products where she was to give the keynote speech. She had stopped by to see me on her way out of town but I was so busy at the time I hadn't paid much attention to her. She wanted me to hear her speech and she followed me around the shop reading it to me. I'm not a judge of good speech-making, I was preoccupied and irritated but too polite to tell her so. Why couldn't she see I was busy, I wondered. In the end she left and called out "Wish me luck!" as she went out the door.

"I thought you said 'Luck is for rabbits!'" I replied, but I don't know if she ever heard me. I would never know.

Millie talked on, talking me through the shock. Jo had run off the road and hit a tree. They thought she probably had a heart attack and died immediately. I wondered what her last thoughts had been. When we rang off, I sat staring out the front window for a long time. I was grieved that Jo was gone. I had barely gotten to know her, and suddenly she was gone. I was overcome once again with a sense of loss and unbearable loneliness, but somehow the tears just wouldn't come.

It was like losing Grama all over again.

It was probably shock, and denial.

Maybe I was finally numb to grief.

The funeral was held on Wednesday and we were all there. Jo's son, Jeremy, and his wife had flown with her body back to Clareville. I'd never met them before and it was a terrible time to first meet anyone, when they are grief-stricken.

It should always rain at funerals. It seems an abomination when the sky is a hot laughing blue. Most of the town turned out for the graveside service. A lot of people knew Jo. This shouldn't be happening, I thought miserably. On a sunny day like this, we should be having a picnic. I looked around at the black-clad mourners, Ivy, Millie, Ruth, Viola and the rest. Some of the fidgety younger children had a hard time understanding the solemnity of the occasion and that a beautiful summer day was not a time to romp in the grass between the gravestones.

No one ever seems to know what to do afterward. For a while I went to the reception at her house and paid my respects to her family but without Jo being there I didn't feel comfortable in her space. I left and went to my shop, although I didn't know what I was going to do there. I felt listless and adrift, and when I approached the front door and my hand-written "Closed for Funeral" sign. I threw up my hands in dispair and walked across the park and through the gate to Ivy's. Her lights were off and the blinds were down but the front door was open so I went inside. My eyes had a hard time adjusting to the gloom after the bright sunshine. But then a voice called out, "Back here," and I followed it to the alcove where I had first met the Wombats. Ivy and Millie were sitting at the same table only this time they were wearing their best black, Millie in a knock-off Givenchy and Ivy in JC Penney. Despite their differences, here they were together. They're an odd pair, I thought affectionately, but friends nonetheless.

"You can hang your hat there if you like," Millie said, pointing to an old wooden hat stand where theirs already hung. I added mine and wearily sat down. They were sipping from tall green frosted glasses. Between them was an empty chair with a glass sitting on it, full and untouched.

"You look awful, love," Ivy said. "You haven't slept, have you?" I shook my head. She stood up and went to the kitchen.

I was silent. It was hot and airless in the restaurant and I took off my suit jacket and hung it on the coat rack. It was the only black outfit I owned. I hate the color. I've worn it too often and never wear it by choice.

"You okay?" Millie asked. Ivy returned and placed a green glass in front of me.

"Yeah," I finally sighed. "It's just that too many people have died on me. My mother died when I was twenty. Then Jack, Grama and now Jo."

"She didn't do it on purpose, you know," Millie joked, perhaps trying to lighten up the dark mood.

I smiled weakly and took a sip. It was a very strong mint julep.

A voice called out from the front door. "We thought we'd find you here. Watch your step here, Viola." Marlene and Viola were silhouetted in the doorway. Marlene had her hand under Viola's elbow and guided her into the gloomy restaurant. They joined us at the table. Ivy pointed to the hat rack and they added their black veiled hats to the growing collection. Marlene hung Viola's cane from a hook. The rack began to look like a depressed scarecrow or a mannekin with a bad attitude.

"It's so hot," said Viola, fanning herself as she sat down. "Could I have some cold water, Ivy?"

"Of course, love," Ivy replied and stood up to fetch it. She stumbled slightly as she did so and it occurred to me that perhaps she and Millie were ahead of us, already on their second drinks. Or third.

"Well, here we all are," Marlene commented as she loosened the wide belt which had kept her cinched together for the last few uncomfortable hours. "Whew!" she breathed with relief. "Ex-

cept for Ruth," she observed. "Ivy! While you're up, call Ruth
and tell her to get on over here."

"Alrighty," Ivy called cheerfully from the kitchen. Ice cubes
clunked and a tap ran, filling the silence around us. A minute
later she emerged with cold water for Viola and three more green
glasses, and said, "Ruth will be right over. She says there's no one
in the beauty shop anyway."

Millie and I were silent while we sipped our drinks. Marlene
fussed over settling Viola into her chair until Viola finally slapped
her hands away, irritable from the heat. A minute later Ruth
trotted into the restaurant.

"What did you do, run all the way over?" Millie laughed. She
had almost finished her drink, perhaps the effect was beginning
to show. I took another sip.

Ruth puffed her way toward us. She headed for the empty chair
between Ivy and Millie but Millie waved her to another chair
where she flopped down, wiping beads of sweat from her brow
with the back of her hand. Ivy pushed a drink toward her.

"It's so hot," Viola repeated. Her hand tembled as she sipped
her water. "Why do people have to die on such hot days?" Then
she picked up her julep and downed half of it right off.

"Bloody inconsiderate, isn't it?" Millie said bitterly with another slightly unhinged laugh. It was definitely the julep. But
even under the influence of alcohol, Ivy and Millie couldn't seem
to get together. The bourbon mellowed Ivy out into a floating
serenity. Millie was morose. "Here's to Jo." She raised her glass
but didn't drink. The rest of us did. Even Marlene, who scrunched
up her face at the taste but said nothing.

"Phfatt!" Ruth spat. "What is this?"

"A mint julep," Ivy explained. "Mostly straight bourbon."

"Yech," Ruth replied.

"It was Jo's favorite drink," Ivy pointed out quietly. "Millie
thought—"

"Oh," Ruth fell silent. "Oh," she repeated and bravely took
another gulp.

We drank in silence. The strong bourbon began to spread a warm tingling sensation from my stomach, up through my chest and out toward my fingertips. I realized I hadn't eaten anything since the day before.

"It seemed appropriate," Ivy continued to explain in her soft British accent.

The bourbon and the heat took an even quicker toll on Viola. Her head bobbed listlessly and she nodded off to sleep with her chin on her chest. Her hands lay crumpled limply on her lap and a slight old woman's snore rattled gently out of her.

Marlene laughed. "Hey Vi! You're not going to be the next one to conk out on us, are you?" But Viola didn't stir. Millie reached for Viola's glass. Holding her manicured fingers across the top of it, she siphoned the remainder of the drink through the tinkling ice cubes into her own glass. Now there's something you don't see Boston ladies do very often, I thought. Her action made me want to giggle but I suppressed it.

"Might know Jo would drink something like this," Marlene commented, stirring her finger in her tall glass. "Nobody drinks these anymore, do they?"

"Maybe she just had to be different," Ivy offered out loud.

"She *was* different," Millie giggled. I'd never seen Millie tight before and it surprised me. Ivy giggled too, but at least she had the sense to be embarrassed and cover her mouth with her hand, stiffling it. I remembered my mother used to say, "If there's something wrong with you, get over it as quickly as possible. If you can't get over it, pretend you have. If you can't pretend you have, don't show up. If you do show up, you should at least have the decency to feel ashamed."

Now why did I think of that just then.

I took another drink. You could get used to the taste of these things, I thought.

"That silly little car of hers," commented Marlene. "Lady Bug versus a tree. She didn't stand a chance!"

"She drove too fast," I said.

"She did everything fast," Ruth pointed out. "No 'stop and smell the roses' for her."

"Maybe she felt there were a lot of things she wanted to get done," I said, defending my friend.

"She should have known better," Millie said and everyone nodded.

"What do you mean?" I asked.

"Her heart, you know," Ivy answered.

"She had a bad heart?" I asked in surprise. Why hadn't anyone told me? Then I remembered her doctor's appointment. But she had passed it off as if nothing was wrong.

"No. Not really," Millie explained. "She had rheumatic fever when she was a child."

"It can weaken your heart," Ivy continued.

"The doctor was always telling her to slow down and relax more, but you know Jo. Wouldn't listen," Ruth added.

"I had no idea!" I exclaimed. It seemed as if I was the only one surprised by Jo's death.

"She had to do everything her way, of course," Marlene complained. "Did you know that I painted her portrait as a housewarming when she bought that big new house of hers? She foisted the painting on her son Jeremy to hang in his office. He relegated it to the lobby."

"She loved that picture!" I exclaimed. How could Marlene have misinterpreted Jo's actions so badly? "And Jeremy told me he was so proud of his mother that he wanted everyone to see her painting by hanging it in the lobby! How can you say such things," I blurted out, and started to cry. I put my face in my hands.

"Yeah, how dare we trash her, eh?" Marlene said sarcastically. I sobbed in the silence.

"Because sometimes she was a pain in the butt—" said Ruth.

"But she was always our friend," Marlene finished.

"Because we loved her," Millie said quietly.

I looked at Millie and there were tears in her eyes which she refused to let fall. I sat up again and leaned back in the chair exhausted. The bourbon and my hot anguish made me sweat in the already stifling heat. I was awash in fluid from every pore.

There was a long silence as we stared at the checkered table-cloth. We were a circle of hands, an anatomy of women. Age spots, scars and callouses. Arthritic knuckles, thin or pudgy fingers wearing diamond rings or simple gold bands, watches, bracelets. Crepey skin, blue veins, moist palms. Deep-creased lifelines, broken heartlines. Capable hands that could rock a cradle, take a temperature, sooth a brow, wipe away a tear, make love, make lunch. Not a single hand that could hold back a friend for even a moment from death's grasp.

"I never got to say goodbye," I sighed. "Not properly." It bothered me that our last meeting had been so abrupt. I had been so inattentive to Jo's needs.

"None of us did, love," Ivy pointed out, and put her hand gently on my arm. "No one ever does."

She was right. They had all known Jo longer than I had. Why did I think my own personal grief was the most overwhelming and important? I pulled myself together, wiping the tears from my face.

"I guess if your own friends can't trash you, who can?" I smiled weakly.

I raised my glass to the empty chair. "To Jo." Everyone raised theirs.

"It was a lousy death," Marlene said.

"It's a lousy drink," Ruth said.

"You were a lousy friend," Millie said.

"Goodbye, Jo," I said softly.

"I wish I could remember the name of the poet who said: 'And if the earth has forgotten you/Say to the still earth: I am flowing/To the rushing waters say: I am,'" Ivy quoted. We turned to look at her in surprise. She waved us away with a dissembling gesture. "British private school education," she explained with a blush, "But it was a long time ago."

We finished our drinks and then Ivy stood up. The rest of us did the same. Ivy suddenly hurled her glass at the back wall where it crashed and shattered. It was her own wall. None of us would have thought of it. At the sound, Viola trembled and snorted but didn't stir. Immediately afterwards, the rest of us followed in unison. With that loud shattering Viola awoke with a start. Seeing us standing, she assumed everyone was getting ready to leave. "Meeting adjourned!" she said.

"Well put," said Millie, and we all laughed.

THE SATURDAY OF LABOR DAY weekend had been a sultry hot day and it didn't look as though the evening was going to provide any relief. We held our usual Saturday afternoon quilting class but it was subdued and listless without Jo's vitality. The store was busy all day, and I was grateful for that. It kept me from missing her too much. She had been my mentor in town and friend in adversity. I'd never fill the hole she left behind.

Joyce was run off her feet all day. Beads of sweat trickled down her neck and dampened her shirt in our un-air-conditioned shop, so I sent her home early. Susan and Jennifer were at a pool party and Hobbes hadn't stirred from his day-long doze in the only cool darkness he could find—the tile floor in the storage room. So I was alone in the shop just before closing time. I was straightening up and returning bolts of fabric to their color-coordinated places when the shop suddenly grew dark. At first I thought the lights had gone out but then I realized that intense black clouds had abruptly blown in from the West, from behind the building where I hadn't seen them coming.

"Ah, maybe rain," I said hopefully, "and relief." I finished with the shelf I was working on and then walked over to the open front door. I got there just as a forewarning rush of wind tore up the street, pushing litter and dust in front of it. The Main Street shoppers had gone home to dinner so there were few cars parked in the street. Over in the park, the sudden blast of wind caught the trees and throttled them fiercely. They scarcely had time to roll up their leaves before the first splatters of rain fell noisily to the ground and the first boom of thunder rattled the windows. I stood in the sheltered doorway watching the unexpected cloudburst and listening to the rain beat heavily on the overhanging tin roof. The eaves trough quickly filled and a cascade of water crashed to the pavement beside my terracotta pots of geraniums. I took a deep breath of cool air and relaxed.

A banging from the back of the shop reminded me that I had left the rear door open all day trying to catch any breezes. It was slamming against the building as I hastened to bolt it against the rain, getting splattered as I did so. Then I stepped quickly back to the shopfront. I didn't want to miss any of the storm. I was walking head down, brushing water from my hair and arms as I approached the door and almost ran right into Daniel. He came dashing through the downpour into the shop.

"Oh," I exclaimed in surprise as he grabbed me by the arms to avoid bumping into me. He dropped his hands and we stepped apart.

"Sorry," he apologized.

"It's okay." I laughed. "I wasn't looking where I was going."

"Some storm," he said uneasily, not sure whether he was welcome or not. His shirt was soaked and steam oozed from the wet spots of his body as we stood awkwardly in the doorway. A crack of lightning followed almost immediately by an explosion of thunder boomed directly overhead. Then, as if to emphasize that the storm was right over us, the rain pummeled down harder.

"Yes," I agreed, and leaned against the doorframe, staring wistfully out into the rain. "I love storms," I said. "Ever since I was a little girl."

Daniel just nodded and we gazed out into the wall of water filling the street. A long pause fell between us. The thunder rumbled over the park and beyond.

"Aggie. I'm sorry," he said finally.

I turned to look at him quizzically. I didn't know what he was apologizing for.

"I'm sorry about Jo," he explained. "I didn't know. I just heard. I've been away fishing and I just got back today. I came right over."

"It's okay. There's nothing you could have done." I looked away. My throat burned as I held back my tears.

He shrugged. "I could have been here," he said gently.

I looked back, into his eyes. We gazed at each other for a long moment, the sound of rain pounding in my ears. I glanced down, not knowing what to say, pursing my lips together to keep my chin from trembling. Daniel reached out his hand and cupped it gently around my elbow as if to steady me. Then I leaned into him with a sigh as he wrapped his arms around me. I started to cry. He held me for a long time as the thunder boomed and the rain fell. My heart ached and my tears rolled. I wept in his embrace, and within the circle of his arms I smelled fresh air, laundry soap and cologne, and a man's skin. It was soothing. It was like going home.

"I'm sorry," I apologized between sobs. I tried to push myself away from him, resisting the feelings, but he tensed his hold and kept whispering, "It's okay, it's okay," as he stroked my hair softly.

In a few minutes I gathered myself together. Once I stopped crying, it was embarrassing to be in his embrace. I lifted my head from his chest and tried to laugh over my burst of emotion. I brushed his shirt, saying, "Well, if it wasn't wet before, your shirt's sure wet now!"

He gave a so-what shrug without letting go his hug and grinned. "You're beautiful when you cry," he teased.

"Oh sure," I replied sarcastically, rubbing my finger under my eyes where I was sure my mascara had smeared. Outside, the sudden deluge abated and the thunder rolled away. We looked into each other's eyes again for a long heartbeat and then he kissed me. It was soft and sweet and new, and it felt good; so I kissed him back and we lingered in it while the rain slowed. A drop of water fell from his wet hair, ran down his nose and onto my cheek. As we stepped apart a blue van came splashing up the street to the curb in front of the shop, behind Daniel's truck.

"It's the girls," I said as I recognized my car. The rain had obviously ended their barbeque. I ran my hands through my hair and wiped them over my face, tidying up.

Daniel took another step backward, embarrassed. "I'm sorry," he said quickly before they had a chance to pile out. "That was forward of me, Aggie. I took unfair advantage—"

I shook my head. "Not to worry," I assured him. Susan ran laughing to the doorway between the last droplets of rain. The sky lightened again and the moment passed away between us.

ALL THE QUILT BLOCKS I made so far had been traditional patterns and an impulse seemed to be compelling me toward something different. I cast about for inspiration, but as I thought back on the month that had passed the only idea that kept coming to me were the words "summer storms." At first I didn't know what they meant. They rolled around in my head for a couple of days until I realized that it was the name of a contemporary Japanese quilt block I'd seen in Nihon Vogue magazine a few months earlier. I immediately knew that it had to be my next quilt block. I love the richness and asymetrical nature of Japanese patchwork quilts. As with most Japanese art there is a whimsical off-centredness to them. They remind me that life is often slightly askew, that predictable regular patterns are interrupted, that balance is not always equal.

In the *Summer Storms* block, two jagged yellow bolts of stylized lightning streak across the square from the top right and left corners down to meet at the horizon, in the middle of the bottom edge. Behind them are curved arcs of gray-black thunderclouds on a clear blue sky background—as if to emphasize how quickly menacing storms blow up in your face. You never know until it has passed whether the wind will bring destruction or healthy rain.

Like the lightning, Jo had disappeared. A shining new friendship had been shattered in a moment. The rumble of thunder, strong at first, faded away, echoing, soft and softer still.

And in the same flash, another relationship had sparked into existence.

EIGHT

Courthouse Steps

IT WAS FINALLY HARVEST TIME. The fields around town were overflowing with tall corn, fat melons and sweet apples. The smell of wood smoke began to permeate the air and multi-colored leaves started to fall upon the hot dry ground. It was time to reap what had been sown.

The first Council meeting was scheduled for the second Wednesday of September. It came far too soon. I dreaded it. It felt like going back to school after summer vacation. No, it was worse than that. I agonized that we hadn't done enough. There must be more that we needed to do, I thought. A few more names on the petition. More documents to be gathered. For weeks, I had spoken to everyone I could think of about our counter-proposal. I asked Jack's question, "If you were me, what would you do?" And of course, despite Marlene's best efforts, the Preservation Order still had not arrived. I know we had done everything possible and despite Jo's death, the Wombats were raring to go into battle. I was ready to do my part. But there must be more we could do. So much was riding on council's decision.

On the day of the fateful council meeting, a wrecking ball was parked symbolically in front of the cornerstone house, waiting menacingly in the overcast evening gloom. AJ wasn't going to waste any time when the gavel came down on the vote. Like Humpty Dumpty, all the king's horses and all the paper in the world wouldn't put Armbruster's headquarters back together again once the building fell.

That evening followed another hot and airless day. Even the birds had given up singing in the heat as I walked slowly across

153

the park toward the town hall. I wondered what Dalton Rimple, Clareville's first mayor, would think of everything that was happening. I was sure he had battled for the park, thinking it would stand forever as his bequest to all the unknown generations of the future. I passed through the southern gate, the gate of high noon and action, the gate of the Coyote, and wondered if the old trickster was going to pull some magic on us. The gray granite steps of the town hall rose in front of me. There were only ten steps but they felt like a hundred. My legs had turned to lead. I felt as though I were climbing the Lincoln Memorial. What would the Great Emancipator have said about the judgement we were seeking tonight, I wondered. I was reminded of the *Courthouse Steps* quilt block design and on an impulse I decided that no matter what the outcome it would be my next quilt block. How appropriate. A courthouse, like the town hall, is where you go to seek justice. Whatever the decision would be, some sort of justice would be served tonight.

The *Courthouse Steps* pattern, strangely, is a variation of the *Log Cabin* block that has been popular since before the time of Abraham Lincoln and his log cabin. It is an appropriate reminder that even though Lincoln was ultimately to lead the country through one of its most terrible periods of history, Lincoln himself was a dismal failure at almost everything else he tried until he was elected president. From such humble log cabin beginnings comes the justice of the American courthouse.

The *Courthouse Steps* block is made by sewing increasingly longer strips of fabric on two sides of a small central square. By shading each strip dark to light, an illusion of perspective is created, like stairs rising up in front of your eyes. It's a very balanced block design, I reflected, the way justice should be balanced, with common sense logic on one hand and compassion for the common man on the other.

I went to the meeting early to get a good seat, but by seven o'clock the town hall was already filling up fast. I tried to think strategically, what would Jo want us to do? Sit in the front row this time, or otherwise? I decided to have our group sit in the middle of the hall to one side. We staked out three rows of seats and Jennifer stood in the middle watching the door. She waved people to her as she spotted fellow supporters. Soon we had a solid block of backers all around us. We seemed to be "among the people" and it felt reassuring.

Ivy and Susan were stationed at the door handing out cardboard buttons that said "STOP" with a green ribbon attached. By the time the meeting started, there was a reassuring sea of green ribbons in the hall. But were there enough, I worried. At our last Wombats meeting Jo had insisted we should dress in green when the time came and in her honor we had done that. She had an instinctive flair for drama and it made me wonder how colorful her Board meetings at JoBelle Products must have been when she was manouevering for policies she wanted to instigate. Even though she had been "mostly retired" for several years, I'm sure her presence in the company was missed there too. When she originally suggested it, I thought wearing green was a dumb overly-theatrical idea and a silly psychological ploy. (Besides I don't look good in green. Years ago, when avocado was in fashion, I bought green bedsheets—but they made Jack and me look like corpses. We didn't make love for three months, until I finally threw them out.) However, looking around the council hall, I was reassured because it looked as though "the greens" had a lot of champions. The Wombats were all in green, and each of us wore a black ribbon in memory of Jo.

Some of the support was unintentional, and humorous. I laughed when I saw that Frank Dempsey, one of the council members, inadvertently wore a green sweater that evening. It looked as though he and several others were in our camp, even though we strongly suspected they weren't. When he realized his sartorial error, he quickly took his sweater off, hung it on his chair and spent the chilly air-conditioned evening in his shirtsleeves, looking unhappier than usual.

I saw Daniel across the room on the far side. He was wearing a casual black and beige plaid shirt but he had two of our "green" buttons on his chest with two more stuck on his baseball cap. He smiled and lifted his cap when he saw me looking. I was glad he was there. For some reason it gave me a sense of security to know he was supporting our movement. I felt like a maiden at a Medieval Fair—my troubador was in the lists, and he was wearing my colors.

Unfortunately, the enemy camp had taken up position three rows directly in front of Daniel. As before, AJ was neatly dressed and looked all the world like an earnest young businessman. Under other circumstances he would have been the kind of young man you would welcome into your home as a potential son-in-law. You know, the little things you look for. His shoes were polished and he stood up politely to shake hands with his elders.

Shake your head, girl. This isn't a pup back from obedience school. As my grandfather would have said, this is the Big Bad Wolf of Bloor Street in sheep's clothing, huffing and puffing at your door, about to blow it in! Having compassion for the world doesn't mean you go blind or that you become shark-bait, or that you don't take a stand when you know something is wrong. Compassion is not about being a doormat to a bully. Trust in people but read the fine print and ask the questions that haunt you. Don't sign until you are satisfied. Okay, okay.

Al Junior sat flanked by several men in dark blue suits wearing humorless faces, executive length socks, and shine-like-mirrors city shoes. Money was obviously serious business to them. What they lacked in team vivacity they made up for with an air of power and authority. They had the confidently scary air that all bankers have. The big boys were uniformly pre-middle age young lions still hungry for success. Our town bank manager, twenty years their senior, sat in the row behind, perhaps not quite in bed with them, but with his hat firmly planted in their ring. Even in his best brown suit he didn't quite have the confidence to sit up front with his intimidating potential partners.

Marlene had not arrived by the time the meeting started. She had decided to drive to the capitol to see what she could do in person about obtaining the Preservation Order, even at the eleventh hour. But there was no sign of her yet.

The pit of my stomach sank lower and lower, faster and faster as we labored through the routine business portion of the meeting. I didn't even register whatever else was on the agenda. When the Clerk read, "The next item is the town square redevelopment proposal," my stomach hit the floor like an anvil in a cartoon.

The Clerk read Al Junior's proposal in full, then Mayor Al said, "Before we take a vote I will advise the Clerk that due to the nature of this vote, Council members have asked that this be a secret written ballot. Please provide Council with materials. And before Council votes, the Chair calls for discussion from the floor. I will advise you, ladies and gentlemen, that in the interest of time this evening, you will be allowed to speak only once."

That was it. The starting gun exploded and the race began.

It felt as though all eyes turned toward us, the Wombats. There was heavy expectation in the air. I shifted in my seat and started to raise my hand, but Millie held my arm down, which was pretty easy because I had no strength in it anyway.

"You only get one chance," she whispered. "Let the hotheads talk first." And sure enough, the split-second of hesitation was enough.

"Mr. Mayor!" came a demanding voice from the other side of the room. George Albert waved his hand vigorously. Every head turned in his direction and he got the nod.

"It's obvious to everyone with half a brain that this town needs fixing. Your boy Al there has done a fine job putting together this new plan. He's got money from a reputable development company just ready to be given to us. Why, they wouldn't be interested at all if it wasn't a profitable idea," he proclaimed.

Sally Smith jumped up and without waiting for the official nod, exclaimed, "Profitable to who? Them, not us. You're a fool if you think they're doing this out of the goodness of their hearts. They don't care a penny about this town!"

Yeah, yeah, right, rustled half the crowd, growing excited. The buttons on Daniel's cap bobbed up and down.

"Who needs a bunch of old trees and a park nobody uses," George continued, ignoring Sally.

Yeah, yeah, right, rustled the other half of the crowd. But the buttons on Daniel's cap shook back and forth, no.

Tap, tap, tap went the gavel. Another hand waved, and got the nod.

"It's all very well to be sentimental about the trees in the park, but the only logical course has to be based on economic realities. The park is valuable and expensive real estate which should be put to better use," someone said.

Right, right, went that annoying other half of the room. No, no went my loyal cap.

Tap, tap, tap went the gavel again. And again. Each time, someone rose to their feet to express an opinion. The debate slammed back and forth. But individual opinion was not going to change anything, and it added nothing new, except vigor, to the subject.

I had learned something from my last Council meeting, and as each person spoke, I didn't watch the speaker. I watched the crowd, trying to take its temperature. I soon lost Daniel's cap in my search for consolation from public concensus. I tried to judge how many heads nodded for, or against, in the hope that Council members were also watching the sea of impassioned faces in front of them. Would it influence them at all?

I glanced over and noticed that Marlene's seat was still empty. Not a good sign. But just as I was adding another ulcer to my worries, the door opened and Marlene sidled in. She groped her way quickly between the standees and the extra chairs, down the side aisle, and as Ruth moved over she came to rest beside me.

"Where are we at?" Marlene asked breathlessly. Thumbs up, she indicated. It started to feel like an eleventh hour courtroom drama scene. The door opens and Paul Drake rushes to Perry Mason with the final nail on the coffin, so to speak. My nerves were so frazzled that all my metaphors were getting mixed up.

"Go for it," I directed her and she raised her hand and stood up. She waited patiently while Mayor Brown banged his gavel for silence and gave her the floor.

"Your Honor," she started. "I'm sorry I was late to the meeting but I just drove here from the Capitol where I obtained this piece of paper. It may influence what Council decides tonight. It's a Preservation Order, signed by the National Trust, on the Armbruster building. It stipulates that the building is of historical significance and cannot be torn down." She smiled triumphantly as she turned to look at Al Junior who now had murder in his eyes. The wrecking-ball was now headed toward him.

A cheer went up from the greens.

Mayor Al looked stunned. Council members followed his lead and looked stunned too, and then turned to each with questioning glances and shrugs that said, "What does this mean?"

There was an astounded murmuring in the hall as everyone asked their neighbors the same question.

Al Junior went into flurried conference with the big boys who looked uniformly unhappy. He was fervent. They were clearly annoyed. The big boys don't like surprises. Evidently, Al Junior had made a tactical error in not warning them of this possibility. Lesson Number One, son, always operate on a "no-surprises" basis.

Finally, Councilwoman Rita Appleton waved her hand at Al Senior and asked, "What does this mean to the proposal, Mr. Mayor?"

Mayor Al pointed his gavel at Al Junior who leaped to his feet. "Not a thing, Sir, your Honor. The proposal stands. In anticipation of this happening, our architects are already preparing drawings which will incorporate this wonderful old building into the new plan." He bowed toward Marlene with a superior smile on his face.

"Ha! Wonderful old building that until five minutes ago you wanted to tear down!" she retorted.

AJ tried to shrug nonchalantly. "We're prepared to be flexible. If people feel strongly about this building we can easily keep it in the new plan." He laughed, his forced joviality tinged with high-pitched nervousness. "No point getting all hot and bothered just because a bunch of dingbats want to keep an old building," he said under his breath as he sat down.

"That's *Wombats!*" Marlene replied evenly.

"Al, sit down . . . and . . . shut . . . up!" Millie ordered. There was a burst of applause and Al did as Momma told him. If she had to tolerate his business dealings, she did not have to brook his rudeness, not from Millie's boy.

The hall again erupted in uncontrolled discussion and Mayor Al banged sternly with his gavel. The room slowly came back to order as he started to speak. "It would be a private matter between the architects and the development company as to how the Armbruster building is retained and incorporated into the plan, so long as it is retained. A preservation order is a legal instrument that they will have to abide by. If we have confirmation that the redevelopment project can still proceed as proposed," he looked sternly at Al Junior with a tell-the-truth-son glare and AJ nodded vigorously, "then we can proceed on that basis."

"If there are no *new* arguments to be presented," Al Senior looked forlornly and helplessly at Millie, "we will have to call for the—"

"Okay, now!" Millie whispered forcefully and pinched my arm.

"Ow!" My arm shot up in the air.

Mayor Al seemed to sigh with relief and said formally, "A-hm, the Chair recognizes one final speaker from the, er, Wombats." He smiled faintly and it suddenly occurred to me that perhaps Al and Millie had agreed on a signal which was going to allow me to speak last.

All of Jo's encouraging words over the months rang in my ears and I could feel Grama's arm around my shoulder. This was it. In the eternity that passes in the split-second of terror, I saw the last few months flicker again before me and what had brought me to this point, this final test. I remembered what I had discovered about the challenge that I had accepted so long ago, and asked myself the questions: Am I still faithful? Have I said "yes" to the challenge and the chaos? Did I tap every resource? Has my compassion for the world allowed me to see clearly and move forward with a worthy purpose? If I could affirm every one, I decided, I knew something good would come of this. This was just one final step. I was past fear, past anger, and way past my own self-interest.

All I had to do now was go the distance—do my best. I had taken myself to the limit and stepped beyond.

I rose to my feet.

And then I blacked out.

No, I didn't faint. I mean I don't remember a thing I said after that. From then on my voice seemed to take on a life of its own. I felt as if I were standing outside myself, observing. I no longer owned the process, or the result. Fortunately, Susan was taping the whole meeting so later I could hear my words. She's so organized, sometimes she drives me crazy, but this time I was glad. My voice was so slow and soft that you could hear a pin drop in that hall.

"Your Honor and Council members. I would like to start by saying that the proposal before Council tonight is a good proposal—"

There was a rush of intaken breath. "Whose side is she on?" someone whispered loudly at my apparent betrayal. That certainly got everyone's attention.

I carried on. "If I read the intention behind the proposal correctly then it is a sincere attempt to solve some of Clareville's problems and for that we owe AJ a debt of thanks . . . ."

I glanced at AJ and he looked surprised but smiled smugly and elbowed the big boy next to him. The blue suit was grim and unimpressed.

". . . for bringing this to the attention of the whole town. To solve our problems it seems it was necessary to get everyone focussed on the problem. And AJ did that.

"The fact that he stands to make money on this proposal should not be counted against him. He is in business, just like I am, and the bank is, and so are many others in this room. We are all in business to make a profit or we go out of business, just like this town would go out of business if it didn't receive enough tax dollars to cover its expenses. As a businessman AJ has done well. I hope his family is proud of him."

Jennifer said later that she thought AJ sat there beaming like a conceited pumpkin.

"He is also young and impatient. And as a young man he should not be faulted for lack of vision or for narrowness of approach. The only problem as we see it, is that this proposal is premature and hasn't considered any alternatives. There is always more than one answer to a problem, and always more than one right answer.

"For the past month, we've been asking people around town what they think of the proposal as it stands, and what they would like to see happen. This box contains the surveys we conducted. Susan."

I pointed at Sue to indicate she should take the box to the Clerk.

"The results, in summary, are this. The majority of people indeed want what AJ's proposal suggests—better parking, a profitable town center, and good shopping. No surprise. But surprisingly enough the majority of people also want to keep the park, too. That seems to be a contradiction of purpose and creates a dilemma. But only if you see the standing proposal as the only answer.

"As an alternative, we put together some ideas which also answer the problem, we think in a more constructive and creative manner. Without losing revenue for the town or the businesspeople . . ."

I went on to describe the Wombats' ideas: a five-point plan covering parking, building use, park use, revenue for AJ and the renovations including new footpaths in the park. Every point emphasized the benefits that the idea would produce, just as our Jo had taught me to do.

"We recognize that this is not being presented as a formal

proposal tonight and that it would have to go through proper channels. All we ask is that when you vote tonight you keep in mind that there are viable alternatives available to tearing down the old square.

"When the founders built this town two hundred years ago, they built it for us, and for the generations to come. When we tear it down we are dishonoring our inheritance. And when we ourselves build, we are talking to our children's children. We must be careful what we are saying to them about values and traditions. When we in our youth and haste tear down the values of older generations, how will we feel when we, too, become the older generation and the next youthful impatient generation tears down what we pass on?

"Do we tear things down simply because they are inconvenient to us for the moment? We can build a shopping mall or lay a parking lot in a matter of weeks or months. But if we have a change of heart, it would take seventy years or so to reproduce the trees in the park. There is no equivalent to fast-drying concrete in growing a tree. We need to be very careful about this decision. It is one that is not easy to revoke or undo. Therefore, it is truly a heavy and unenviable responsibility that Council bears tonight.

"There are people in town whose families have made their home in Clareville for many generations, and there are some, like me, who are newcomers. I may be a newcomer to town, but this was my late husband's and his family's hometown. It's my home now, too. There was something that brought everyone here to Clareville in the first place and made us decide to stay. Founding-family or newcomer, we all care deeply about what happens to it. Is Clareville to be another in a long chain of towns that have torn down their inheritance for short-term profit? Or is Clareville to be the first to reclaim the values that this great country was built on by preserving these living symbols of integrity and endurance, these irreplaceable old members of our community?

"President Kennedy spoke in his inaugural address about passing the torch to a new generation of Americans. Let us be sure that the torch we pass tonight is one that stands for preserving the values and traditions of our past and for saving our environment for generations to come.

"Ladies and gentlemen, thank you for your attention."

When I sat down there was dead silence in the hall. Then I noticed a far away whooshing sound rushing in my ears and a wall of noise came crashing into my head. It was my heart starting to beat again and the blood rushing in my ears.

Then a rattle came from the crowd. It was applause. It started with a staccato crack and grew louder. There were interspersed, "yes, yes" and "that's right" calls, too. It grew to a crescendo. Even AJ clapped. He seemed to have momentarily forgotten himself. Even the big boys graciously added short, politically-correct, and polite applause. Daniel had jumped to his feet and led the joyous thunder. I felt the heat of a blush rush to my cheeks.

Mayor Al tapped sharply with his gavel and shifted uneasily in his seat. "Ahem," he cleared his throat as the crowd subsided. "Thank you all," he said, "for your, er, contributions. We will now take the vote."

The town Clerk handed out ballot forms to everyone in silence. The room was in a deadly hush. The six Councillors quickly marked their papers. Too quickly, I thought. Like Perry Mason, I was trying to assess the jury. They were too quick; their minds had already been made up. A quick jury is a hanging jury, it is said. They folded the ballots and handed them back in silence to the expressionless Clerk who handed them over to Mayor Al. He slowly unfolded each ballot one-by-one and called out the vote.

Guilty. Not guilty. Guilty. Not guilty, my head was going. No, no, wrong scene.

"For," he called out. All the Wombats drew in a sharp breath. Oh no.

"Against." We held our breath.

"Against." We breathed out.

"For." We all drew in another desperate breath.

"For" Oh, no.

Al dropped the last ballot, fumbled as he picked it up and read, "Against." He looked aghast.

Whew! We breathed, thank heaven.

"Oh, oh," said Millie and shook her head with a look of despair on her face.

"What?" I asked. "It's a tie. Three-to-three. Do they vote again?"

"No," she explained. "The Mayor casts the deciding vote in any tie vote."

"Oh," I said, and then looked back at Mayor Al. "Oh, oh." I repeated Millie's foreboding words when I realized what it meant. I was afraid to turn and look at her again but I could feel her tension beside me. I could feel her sitting ramrod straight in her chair. There was an electric energy coming from her, I didn't have to see her to feel it.

Mayor Al began explaining formally in a droning voice, ". . . being the case, the deciding vote is cast by the office of the Mayor." He spoke slowly and painfully, trying to stall for time, probably hoping lightning would strike him either dead or with a brilliant solution that would get him off the hook. As he spoke he shuffled every paper in front of him into a pile on his left, and then shuffled them back to the right again. It was sublime irony that it was finally up to our non-decisive mayor to cast the final vote. Or perhaps his own dragon of destiny had caught up to him at last. He had been sitting on a picket fence long enough and his rear end was about to get the point.

". . . considering all sides in the manner and with the best interests of the whole town in view, I find I must vote..."

Beside me I heard Millie whisper softly, "Be a hero, Al," and my heart broke for her. Here was the sum of this wonderful woman. With all her heart, over and above what she herself wanted, she wanted her husband to do what was right, what he needed to do. There was great love in that fierce whisper.

". . . to oppose the motion before Council," Al exhaled, and all the air seemed to go out of him with the effort it took to speak out at last and take a stand.

There was a momentary silence, then pandemonium broke out. The "greens" all jumped up as one and started hugging everyone in sight.

"We won!" they cried. "We won! We won!"

In my astonished disbelief, at first I couldn't grasp what had happened. After months of anticipation and speculation and turmoil, my brain had gone into neutral. Between the gyrating bodies around me, I stared at Mayor Al. The room seemed to disappear into an eerie tunnel and the din receded to a distant rumble. Then in the bubble of unearthly silence I saw Grama standing behind Al's chair. She had her arm draped casually over the high back and was nodding her head happily. I clearly heard her say, "Everybody won." And she was right.

I smiled at her. She gestured thumbs-up and grinned.

Then Grama put her hand in the air and gave me a little wave. "See ya', Sweetie," she said simply.

"Oh no!" I cried and stuffed two knuckles into my mouth to stifle my tears. In a flash I understood everything. It was the first time I knew she wasn't coming back again. She had never waved goodbye before. "No, wait! I always thought you—"

"You'll be okay," she said gently. "You don't need me anymore. Not that you ever really did, and besides Uncle Bernie needs me now. He's got cancer bad. You'll get the call next week." And with that she simply faded away. No long farewell, just suddenly gone.

The town hall rushed back into full volume. Jennifer and Susan were dancing up and down, drawing circles in the air with their fists and making "woof, woof, woof," noises. "Way to go, Mom!" they cried. I stood still in the pandemonium, suddenly alone.

"Wait for what, Mom?" Susan asked loudly over the noise. I shook my head and brushed away the tears from my eyes and hugged her. Everyone thought I had just been overcome with the emotion of victory. I exhaled a trembling breath as I let my angel go. Then I remember smiling as I felt the joy in the room engulf me. I let myself be carried away by it as we hugged and yelled.

NINE

Variable Stars

AS THE JOYOUS DIN CONTINUED to erupt around me, I turned to look at Millie and saw that she alone remained seated, still and focussed. There were tears in her eyes. Tears of joy, relief and pride. She was gazing at her husband and smiling a small private smile and nodding her head, nodding reassurance.

I glanced back at Mayor Al where he had slumped to one side in his high back swivel chair, looking tired. I hoped that later, in retrospect, he would see this turning point as a personal triumph, even though now it was obviously a terrible strain. His gavel dangled listlessly in his hand. Perhaps he was thinking about the votes he was going to lose in the next election. Until that moment I think Al had truly enjoyed being mayor of Clareville. He was gazing at Millie and a small weary smile played at his mouth. He shook his head slightly as if saying "I can't believe I did that." Across the noisy room their eyes were locked in shared triumph, and pain. Al sighed, shrugged his shoulders, and broke the silent spell. He turned his attention to his son, who was leaning sideways talking to the big boys.

The rest of Council grew uncomfortable and restless. Finally, Al went tap, tap, tap with the gavel.

"Ladies . . ." he said. Rap, rap, rap, he tried with more vigor. "Ladies and gentlemen," he called out uselessly.

The town Clerk finally stepped forward, took the gavel and wham! wham! wham! yelled, "Quiet!" above the crowd.

We sat down, and slowly and reluctantly came back to order as Mayor Brown watched his son in glum conversation with the big boys who were shaking their heads "no" to something. Then they got up and left. AJ was deserted, sitting alone in his row. Even the bank manager had sidled uneasily to a more distant seat. AJ looked as though he had just lost his first little league baseball game and needed his Dad. But Dad had bet on the other team.

"Thank you, ladies and gentlemen," Al was going through the formalities. "If there is no other business to be brought before Council—"

Pierre LaBouche suddenly stood up and raised his hand. "Monsieur," he said, and Al nodded toward the wiry Frenchman.

"Mesdames, et monsieurs, if ze wonderful lady, Ivy, weeshes to open a cafe in ze park, then I, Pierre LaBouche of LaBouche Freres vineyards weesh to offer to the young sir, AJ, to open a fine wine bar in heez stone building on ze square. What may be one small step for Pierre LaBouche may be one great leap for Clareville!" he exclaimed.

"Monsieur LaBouche, this has nothing to do with town Council. You see . . ." Mayor Al said gently.

Surprisingly, it was Frank Dempsey who interrupted, saying, "But it does have to do with the town square. Let's hear this."

"Merci, sir, " Pierre bowed toward Frank and continued. "And my friends Gail and Michael who run ze Quilt Inn are also interested. We have talked over ze wonderful idea tonight and zey weesh to open a fine restaurant on ze ground floor." There were nods of agreement from the two people sitting beside him.

"Good idea," someone commented.

"A decent upscale restaurant in town would be good for tourist trade," another added. I winced at the comment and looked over at Ivy but she was smiling happily, apparently unperturbed by the slight to her own establishment.

"There's some tenants for you, AJ. You may make money from the deal yet," Daniel called out to good-natured laughter.

"Provided, of course, adequate parking can be arranged, such as a fine parking lot between ze stone house and ze Armbruster place as ze Wombat ladies have suggested," Pierre added a codicil to his intention.

Marlene stood up and addressed AJ gently. "AJ, this may be

small consolation but there's good news in the Preservation Order. If the Armbruster building is assessed worthy, there may be funds available to renovate it into a paying museum." An approving rustle passed through the crowd.

Then Ruth stood up and announced, "The downtown merchants formed an association and thanks to Mr. Ming Pak," she gestured toward Mr. Pak who bowed toward us in return, "We've put together a consortium of financial backers who are interested in underwriting the renovation of the shops on the square." Applause followed. "That would include your buildings too, AJ, if you want."

Mr. Winslow of the bank looked stunned at the news. He blustered, "Well, now Ruthie, you don't want to rush into anything. Not with a bunch of strangers. We should talk about this proposal of yours. I'm sure we can do something for you."

Marlene nudged me. "See, I told you he'd come around," she said smugly.

"Mr. Winslow," Ruth replied. "Do you know the story of The Little Red Hen? You didn't want to plant the seeds, till the field, nourish, harvest or grind the grain, but now you want a slice of our bread? Yes, we can talk but you'd better have some jam up your sleeve to put on our bread!" The town laughed. I was glad Ruth had come back into our fold.

"You know, we're the only town for one hundred miles around with a band shell and a park big enough to hold concerts. Why don't we organize concerts? They could draw people from all around. Especially with all the other things happening around the park," the enthusiastic manager of the Fox movie theatre suggested.

"The bandshell is a wreck," someone pointed out. "It needs a new roof and a paint job."

"Well, as President of the Rotary, I can tell you that would be a volunteer project we would consider undertaking. We can provide the manpower, er, person power, if someone else can provide the materials," Chuck Summerhill said.

There was applause for that.

"Well, shoot, I'll donate the paint," offered Frank Dempsey to everyone's surprise. Applause again. Perhaps we had misunderstood him. Perhaps he didn't want the park torn down after all, but simply wanted to see it put to good use.

"And the lumber," called out Curtis Mayes from the lumberyard.

"We could put on plays in the park in the Summer," Megan Perry from the amateur theatre group suggested. Right, right, from the town.

Johnson's Nursery said they would replant the neglected gardens.

It was wonderful to see the town coming together with increasing excitement. The tide had turned. Now there was a flow of goodwill and support from all quarters. It was like an old Andy Hardy movie, where some optimistic soul inevitably stands up, rallying everyone by saying, "We can take this old barn and turn it into a theatre . . ." which gives them an opportunity to sing and dance. I guessed that it was time for me to say it, so I stood up again and waited for silence. Mayor Al tapped the gavel lightly for me.

"I know we're running overtime this evening, and everyone wants to go home, and this can't all be done tonight, so what do we have to do to instigate some of these changes and ideas?" I directed the question to Mayor Al. Oh oh, I was taking charge again.

"We form a subcommittee of Council to study the, um, counterproposal and then make recommendations to Council. If Council approves . . ." Mayor Al answered.

"*When* Council approves," Ruth interrupted to laughter.

"When Council approves," Al corrected himself. "the Clerk issues appropriate licenses, and so on, and away you go."

"Who makes up the subcommittee?" I asked.

"Volunteers usually," Al shrugged.

"She should be on it," Horace Baker, my benefactor, pointed at me. I hadn't seen Horace since the day in my shop when he handed me a "campaign contribution."

There were nods everywhere. I happily gestured my acceptance.

"As AJ is a major landlord on the square, I think he should represent the business interests. He is a shrewd businessman and his input would be invaluable," I suggested and AJ perked up. It seemed like a good idea to put the enemy's power and momentum to better, and more constructive, use.

"Yes. Okay," he said in surprise. He smiled for the first time since the vote had been taken.

"And someone from the merchants' association," Johnson added. "What about Ivy?"

Yes, yes, good idea.

"Okay, then let's get busy right away," I concluded.

"Richard will so note in the Minutes," Mayor Al directed the Town Clerk, who now had a name. Satisfied smiles all around.

"If there is no further business to be brought before Council," Mayor Al paused, "then the meeting stands adjourned." He tapped the gavel lightly and dropped it on the table in front of him in final relief.

Then the mingling started. I was immediately surrounded by a group of mixed "greens" and other well-wishers. There were more offers of "help any way I can." I was congratulated many times. I told everyone that it had been the town that had made this happen. Next year is an election year in Clareville and several people suggested I should run for Council. Using the momentum of this victory could have gained me some short-term power and support. I had a brief second of temptation, but I demurred, telling them I already had enough to keep me busy. It was true and besides I decided that my leadership endeavors would be more appropriately spent in the creative realm of my quilt shop, in the circle of women in my network.

The girls kept hugging me. The victory was a great feeling, but the story wasn't finished yet.

I manouevered around so I could see the Council table. All six Council members stayed after the meeting and moved out into the crowd. I guess we'll never know who cast the three votes in favor of the proposal, but it didn't matter. I hoped the town would have the good grace to leave it alone and move on. Everyone is entitled to a change of heart and I hoped those who had cast the losing votes would eventually come around. I was glad it had been a secret ballot.

Mayor Brown was the last to stand. He slowly made his way toward AJ who remained seated, leaning forward with elbows on knees, tapping a rolled up sheaf of papers in one hand, staring dejectedly at the floor. He was the epitome of despair. Without seeing his Dad approach, he sighed and rose unhappily just as Al made it to his side. Al put his arm around his son's shoulder and then walked him proudly down the center aisle toward the door. There was no doubt to anyone watching that Big Al's gesture said, "this is *my* boy!" But AJ was still avoiding people's eyes by looking at the floor—even though he was nodding his head as Al spoke to him. They made it halfway to the door when Pierre LaBouche accosted AJ, shaking his hand vigorously. He waved Gail and Michael over to join their animated conversation. I saw AJ finally laugh—just before I was hailed myself and had to turn away. It was okay, I'd seen closure all around.

The Wombats had gathered around Millie, and as I joined them I heard Ivy say, "That was tough for Al. Tell him thanks from everybody, okay?"

Millie nodded.

We all hugged and started making appointments to begin working on the new town plan. As we were talking, I suddenly felt a touch on my shoulder. I turned and saw it was AJ. He held out his hand to me and said graciously, "Congratulations, Ma'am. No hard feelings. That was a real good speech you made. Thanks for the nice things you said. And thanks for nominating me. I'll try to be helpful on the committee. Just let me know when you want to meet," he smiled faintly.

"Thank you, AJ. I sure will," I answered and we shook hands warmly.

As he turned away, he almost bumped into Jennifer who had

inadvertently come up beside us. "Hello Jennifer," he nodded with another abashed smile.

"Hi," she replied tersely and turned away. He was left staring at the back of her head with a pained expression on his face.

After a few seconds he recovered. "Ready to go home, Mom?" he said to Millie.

She nodded happily. "You bet."

AJ took her arm and they went off to join Mayor Al, the Hero, Dad. We all watched them go.

Susan dug Jennifer in the ribs. "Nice teeth," she quoted Grama jokingly, but Jennifer just shot her sister a withering look.

"What a nice lad," Viola cooed. She had forgotten his felonious assault on her library materials. "I always said he was such a fine boy," she said, watching after him wistfully. We all turned to look at her in surprise. "Reminds me of my own son."

We stared at her.

"What?" she shrugged. "What did I say?"

What could we say? We all just laughed, and split up to go our separate ways home.

When I turned to my seat to retrieve my sweater and handbag, I was surprised to find a long thin box resting on my chair. I picked it up. The box had a clear cellophane top and inside, carefully nestled in white tissue paper, was a single red rose in full bloom. It was so beautiful and unexpected that it made me suck in my breath in surprise.

"Oh!" I said and looked up, just in time to catch a glimpse of Daniel's baseball cap with our Save The Old Park buttons disappear out the door. STOP, I wanted to call out.

I had the feeling that win or lose, the rose would have been left for me anyway. I opened the box. There was no note inside. There didn't have to be. I picked up the rose and held it to my nose, breathing in its sweet scent. Like the victory that night, it was a heady sensation. Yet victory is not the end, I realized. It is just a starting point, a new beginning.

STOP indeed. I guess I'll have to make a GO button and put it in the shop window. Perhaps now there is time, I thought happily as I gathered the rest of my things.

BACK AT THE NOW SAFE AND SECURE little shop on Main Street, Jennifer, Susan and I settled in to enjoy our ritual bedtime pot of tea. I was totally drained by the emotion of the meeting, and yet wildly excited with relief. At first I didn't pay much attention to what the girls were saying as I searched under the counter for a vase. I took it upstairs, filled it with water, arranged my rose in it and placed it on my dresser. Then I reached up, unfastened the chain and removed the gold locket from around my neck where it had hung for fifteen long years. I kissed it lightly and placed it gently in my jewelry box where it belonged, among my other treasures and mementos. As I descended into the shop again I caught snatches of Jennifer's and Susan's conversation.

"Did you see the look on Frank Dempsey's face when Mayor Al said 'against'? I thought he was going to murder him."

"Yeah, but then he came around and offered to donate paint for the bandshell. So go figure, eh?"

"I feel sorry for AJ," Susan said. "It was his big chance. He must feel like a failure now, especially since his own Dad had to vote against him."

"Well, I don't," Jennifer sniffed.

"Aw, come on Jen, you're just ticked off because you didn't realize that he was 'the enemy' as you called him and you were attracted to him. You just won't admit it. He's your kinda guy really, a business tycoon."

"Hmmm," Jennifer paused at that novel thought.

"Great taste in suits," Susan pointed out, coaxing. "Good build, nice buns. Maybe he's not so bad."

Jennifer sighed, reluctantly agreeing, "Maybe not."

"If I were you I'd keep a close eye on him," Susan challenged. "Like maybe from up close. Real close." Changing the subject, Susan nudged Jennifer. "Wasn't Mom terrific?"

"You bet," Jennifer agreed, which brought them back into focus on me.

"Whatcha thinking, Mom?" Jennifer asked brightly.

"Well, actually I was thinking about the quilt block I'm going to make to commemorate this evening. On the way over to the town hall tonight I decided to make a *Courthouse Steps*. It seemed appropriate since we were going there, in great hopefulness, to seek justice." I described the block for them.

"Yeah. Good idea," they nodded and listened while I continued to explain.

"But now I realize I have to make another one, too. A *Variable Stars* to represent how changing our fortunes seem to be at times. Everything turned on the result of one vote. If Al had supported AJ, what would we be thinking and feeling now?"

"Whatever it would be, Mom, I know you would find a way to make it work out. You're always looking for a win-win. Like Grama used to talk about. Like you did tonight with AJ. You didn't attack him the way everyone else did. You let him save face, so he can get a win out of this too. Now he's ready to help us," Susan pointed out. "You turned an enemy into an ally."

She looked at Jennifer, who ignored her pointed remark.

Instead Jennifer said, "Yeah, Mom. Your 'stars' may be 'variable' as you say, but what you do with them is up to you. When this whole thing started, you could have given up, or left town, or whatever . . ."

"I've had my temptations, you know," I interrupted Jennifer.

"But you chose to stick it out and fight. And now everything's going to be fine," Jennifer continued. "That's why you're such a terrific Mom. Grama would have been proud of you tonight." She came over and put her arm around my shoulder. It always surprises me how tall she's grown to be.

"Gee. Do you think so?" I smiled. "That's nice of you to say. It means a lot." I hugged them both. I already knew what Grama thought.

HOBBES LAY PURRING HAPPILY on my shoulder that night in bed. Like all cat lovers I'm convinced he understands everything that's going on around him, and he knew we were going to be okay. Or maybe it was gratitude because he received an extra, victory bowl of Tuna Delight before bedtime.

I lay there thinking about the *Variable Stars* pattern. The eight-point star design is probably one of the most used, most loved, quilt blocks after the *Log Cabin*. It's simple and easy because it has all straight seams and only two design elements, squares and triangles. Therefore it also has endless variations. There must be thousands of star quilts. I wouldn't be surprised to learn that every single quilter has made at least one. There may be as many star quilts as there are stars in the night sky, every one different, every one bright and beautiful.

It was a star that led three wise men on their journey to Bethlehem. It is a lucky star which celebrates good fortune. Children wish on star light, star bright with hope-filled innocence. Like meteors and comets that are the celestial messengers of faith, sometimes our actions become the message to others, to our village and to our children, that our words cannot say.

There's probably a star in the sky for every person on Earth. Maybe we are all variable, or maybe we are all already written in the night sky. How we come together with other neighboring stars defines how we form our own constellations. Perhaps every star is witnessing the birth of a new universe and every shining victory is a new beginning.

TEN

Tree of Life

IT WAS A SAD END TO THE EXCITING SUMMER when Susan returned to school. She had stayed on until the Council meeting but eventually and reluctantly had to leave. Ironically, Jennifer who had been so desperate to leave, was staying on.

A week after the council meeting, just as I was closing the shop, the Wombats along with Jennifer, came bundling into the shop. I was pleased but surprised to see them. Especially all of them together. Assembled like that, with serious expressions on their faces, they looked like a committee of doom.

"What's up?" I asked with concern. "What's wrong?"

"Nothing," replied Millie. "We just wanted to come and see you now that the dust has settled. There's something we need to do."

"Okay. What's that?" I asked as I continued to tidy up.

"Come here and stop fussing," Millie ordered. I joined them at the cutting table.

"Okay. What's up?" I asked again.

"Since you arrived in town, you've really become one of us," Ivy started.

"You did a great job in saving the old park," Marlene continued.

"We all agreed that you were pivotal in getting things done," Millie said. "It was your passion and your 'voice' that made the difference."

"So we decided, unanimously," Ivy continued.

"To name you Mother Wombat of us all," Ruth finished.

"And we made you this honorary mantle to wear at your official Wombat functions!" Marlene exclaimed.

She unfurled a furry brown shawl and draped it ceremoniously over my shoulders. It was embellished with a silver sequined star on the shoulder and with turquois plastic beads and tassles and feathers. It looked all the world like a Native American ceremonial pelt gone crazy. I expected the mantle to be heavy but was surprised to find that it was warm and light. It seemed to fit me perfectly.

I couldn't help but laugh. "This is wonderful. I don't know what to say," I stammered. "I'm honored, I think. And amazed," I laughed again.

"It's made of genuine fake 'wombat' fur, Mom," Jennifer assured me. "Just to be politically correct."

"The Wombats need an official leader, and you're it," Ruth asserted. Apparently the title was real, the symbolic "mantle" was just for fun.

Despite the jokes and laughter, I was truly touched by their gesture. I knew that underneath the silliness they were being serious. I lost my voice as tears began to well up. All I could do was hug each one of them.

"Thank you. You don't know how much this means to me. I'm honored to be Mother Wombat. I'll try to be a good, um, parent," I choked. I patted the furry collar and after taking several deep breaths I found my voice again, "You've been so kind to me. You welcomed me into your town, and into your hearts. You made it so much easier to accomplish whatever I was able to accomplish. And I thank every one of you for that. I feel so blessed.

"And now I'd like to share something with you," I continued as I pulled out the box that held my completed quilt blocks. "This is what I call my Memory Quilt," I explained. "I started it when I arrived in town as an easy 'sampler' to use in teaching quilting but as I worked on each block it ended up becoming a diary of my life here in Clareville. The events that happened to me were the inspiration for each block. When I first heard about AJ's proposal I was terribly shaken up and as this whole drama unfolded I had to learn a lot of things about myself. So, not only does the quilt contain my memories of this time, it also became my teacher. It really did become a teaching quilt after all!"

Then I told them about the stash of fabric I inherited from Grama. After that I laid out each block and explained how they were symbolic and how the first one, *Grandmother's Garden*, represented the calm-before-the-storm I was in when I arrived in Clareville. I had no idea what I was getting into, but I had operated out of blind faith. The second block, *Crossroads*, depicted the fears and confusion I felt about my unpredictable future in my new life, even though I had said "yes" to it in the first place. Everyone appreciated the symbolism of the stormy *Kansas Troubles* block where my troubles suddenly began and I realized that I had to have the courage to simply hold on until I hit the bottom of the roller-coaster ride.

That had been a turning point. I proudly pointed out the shiny new fabric I used for the *Seven Sisters* block which honored the Wombats, including Jo, without whom I couldn't have done anything. Everyone remembered our topsy-turvy summer when a *Monkey Wrench* was thrown into our plans and the Armbruster papers were lost. In trying to answer Jennifer's anguished question, "when does the struggle end," I realized that my passion for what I was doing was the only thing that gave me the strength to endure. The *Tangled Briars* represented my own darkest feelings of confusion and futility. That was the point when I finally understood I had to have compassion for the world and I came to understand that what I was engaged in was beyond my own small self-interest. I had to find my voice and take a stand for something I believed in. It was as if I had inadvertently been preparing for this my whole life. That realization allowed me to see clearly and forced me to face the trauma of the Council meeting. The *Summer Storms* block signified relationships that begin and end so suddenly, without warning.

I would never forget the *Courthouse Steps* night and the meeting, even though I couldn't remember what I had said! As I was on my way to the meeting, I knew that the only thing I could do was my best, even if it took me to the limit of my doubts and insecurities. Victory for me was symbolized by the *Variable Stars* that fortunes hang on. I realized that the victory was not really the end but just the beginning of further growth.

I enjoyed sharing the quilt blocks and their hidden meanings with my friends. I finished by apologizing that the quilt was not complete and that I was a little stuck on how to finish the top.

Joyce laughed. "Well, thank heavens there was a reason. I never wanted to say anything, but I wondered all this time why you were making these queer blocks, with no apparent connection. And the colors didn't even match, like you were making a sampler or something. Some of us wondered if you really were a quilter! So I'm glad you shared your story."

"It's a wonderful idea, dear," said Viola. "I like the way you used so many of the traditional quilt block designs. It could be a pioneer quilt. Well, not that pioneers would have chosen quite those fabrics. But I'm sure it will be fine when you get the binding on."

I laughed affectionately at her somewhat back-handed compliment.

Then I explained, "At some point it occurred to me that the symbolism of my quilt blocks was like the story of a heroine's journey."

"A what?" Marlene asked.

"A heroine's journey. It's sort of a voyage of discovery, like one of those old folk tales Jo liked to tell where a girl or woman sets out through a mysterious woods or opens a forbidden door and then finds herself in an adventure fraught with troubles and obstacles. It's a metaphorical journey into an undiscovered country or a sacred place of wisdom. On the way she sometimes meets allies in the form of magical spirits or animals that help her. She is often tested and must accomplish some extraordinary feat in order to overcome the adversity and return home to her family or to her spiritual center. She comes back transformed, with power and wisdom."

"You mean like Rumplestiltskin where the girl has to spin a pile of wheat into gold," suggested Ruth.

"Or Sleeping Beauty," Marlene added.

"Or Dorothy in The Wizard of Oz," Ivy suggested.

"Right. Those stories are really classical heroine's journeys," I continued. "And with every block, I discovered the process that the heroine has to go through at each stage in the journey and what she needs to survive." I placed my hand on each of the quilt blocks in sequence on the table, indicating the progress of the journey I had made. It seemed to make perfect sense analyzing it afterward, although at the time, even I didn't know what had been happening to me.

"That's a wonderful interpretation, love," Ivy remarked. "And yet somehow it rings true. It's a journey of self-discovery."

I nodded.

"And having made the journey you can teach it to others. Like Hansel and Gretel, you leave behind a trail of breadcrumbs to mark the path for others to follow," Joyce said.

"I would call it my path of stitches," I commented. "It goes from Innocent Sleep to a Wake-up Call to Action, then to a Descent into Trouble where you cross the Threshold of Endless Struggle. If you're lucky, the hidden hands of Allies come to help you, through the ups and downs, and over the Obstacles where your worthy purpose is questioned and then on to the final Test before you attain Victory."

"What about those of us who don't sew or make quilts?" Marlene asked.

"I don't think that matters so much," Ivy responded thoughtfully. "Aggie's path of stitches could be a metaphor for any woman's life, couldn't it?" she answered Marlene and then turned back to me.

"Why not? I think so," I answered. "Perhaps it's the path of the everyday quilter. Doesn't every woman face challenges that transform her in some way? It could be a new business or—"

"It could be a divorce," Marlene interrupted. "That was definitely a Descent into Trouble for me. Talk about despair and frustration. I thought I was going to be married forever. I found out that Sam was having an affair. It completely ripped my life apart at the seams." She picked up the *Kansas Troubles* block. "This whirling black tornado is exactly what it felt like."

"And how did you survive it?" I asked.

Marlene smiled with a realization. "I held on until I hit bottom! And when this bottom," she slapped her ample behind, "hit bottom, I began to bounce back!"

We all laughed.

"There you go," nodded Millie. "For me it was when my son was born. I had no experience with children, and looking after AJ as a baby was the hardest thing I have ever done. At every stage I thought it was the worst that could happen. I had no preparation for it. My pregnancy was awful. I was sick all the time. The delivery was a horror. And then those *endless* feedings and diaper changes. And the crying and crying and crying. If it wasn't him, it was me! That was a Threshold of Endless Struggle for sure."

It was hard to imagine that cool and unflappable Millie could come unglued but everyone has their trials, and breaking point.

"Well, motherhood sure gets my vote as a heroic adventure!" Marlene interjected.

"I don't have children," Ivy commented, "but I suspect that it was the automatic and natural passion of motherhood, your maternal love, that got you through it," she suggested.

"Gee. With everything that you've said, if that's the case," Jennifer joined in, "then I'm still sitting in Grama's Garden in an Innocent Sleep because nothing like that has happened to me yet! I don't consider anything in my life so far as being dramatic enough."

"That could be, Jen, but I don't think a heroine's journey would necessarily always have to be about earth shattering events," Marlene replied. "Take motherhood again. For the most part, as it's happening day-by-day it seems hectic and humdrum. It hardly seems heroic at all. Maybe for you, Jennifer, college was a heroine's journey. Or your first job."

The rest of us nodded agreement. Perhaps youth is simply when the discoveries or adventures are more obvious but less conscious. We think we stop growing when we're grown.

"It was certainly, what did you call it, transformational," Jennifer agreed.

"It can be about the everyday things in life, too, can't it? And it can start any time in life. Maybe even several times," Marlene finished her thought.

"You mean we have to keep learning the same lesson over and over again?" Ruth asked with a frown. "That would be depressing."

I hated to think what she must be thinking. "Or a succession of new ones," I replied. "Unless we don't answer the Call in the first place. A lot of women never make the journey, or else we keep starting and stopping the same journey. There are always distractions and temptations and worse, rationalizations, which lead us off the path. Sometimes just being tired makes us stop in one of the false green valleys along the road. Refusing the Call to Action keeps us stuck in one place. We have to take a leap of faith out to where the action is if we are going to move forward. And mostly it's fear that stops us from making the leap," I added.

"Fear of what?" Jennifer asked.

"Fear of other people thinking you're crazy," Ivy put in softly. I knew she was thinking of her first husband's unfulfilled dream.

"Fear of losing all your security," Marlene added, remembering her divorce.

"Fear that there's nothing else better out there," Ruth commented. I hadn't met her husband but I sensed she was referring to him. If their marriage was so bad, wouldn't there have to be something better for her, I wondered.

"Fear that you'll make an unforgivable mistake," Millie said finally, echoing the worry of every parent.

"Fear of the pain," Jennifer added her insight.

There was a long silence that followed Jennifer's admission.

"But there's pain if you stay where you are," Ruth pointed out. Was she talking to herself or Jennifer, I wondered.

"Every new beginning implies an end of something old," I continued. "And every end involves pain. Pain of separation, pain of loneliness. To go on the journey means to anticipate pain and that can literally scare someone off. But all those fears, when you boil them down, represent only two simple things—the fear of death and the fear of being alone. We fear other people's opinion because we think they will abandon us. We fear losing our security because we think it will ultimately lead to our death, or worse, that we will end up destitute bag ladies—a living death. But our middle of the night, worst-case scenarios rarely ever come true."

"You really can't avoid pain in your life," Ivy commented. "Whether you go on the journey or not, there will be pain. You can't afford to, what did you call it, Refuse the Call."

Yes, I thought, Ivy is probably the bravest one of us here. She never said no to the struggles and challenges. "I've often felt such empathy for you, Ivy," I told her. "I know how it feels to lose a beloved husband. It's such a tragedy that your first husband died without realizing his dream. You had to carry on for him. And now your second husband is an invalid that you have to look after. He's so lucky to have someone as courageous as you."

"But you don't understand, love" she replied quietly. "George is my life. He may be an invalid, but he is far from being in-*valid*. He is my inspiration, my encouragement, my soul mate. I didn't marry his body, I married his soul. For the little care I give him, I receive much more in return. I'm the one who's lucky to have him in my life."

There was another surprising and heartening thing about Ivy. Little did she need my pity.

"Maybe sometimes you don't have the choice to Refuse the Call," Jennifer commented. "That Wake-up Call you referred to could be something like being fired, or breaking up with your boyfriend, couldn't it?"

"Sure," I nodded. "A lot of the time we are cast unwillingly into the journey."

"Oh oh," Jennifer laughed. "Then I guess I'm on one of your heroine's journeys after all!"

Ivy said softly, "There's a line from T.S. Eliot that goes, 'I have always known that at last I would take this road but yesterday I did not know that it would be today.' Perhaps if we knew yesterday what we know today, we would take the road more willingly. Or at least with more awareness."

We paused to reflect on her insight.

"Of course the journey could be about work, or about relationships," I confirmed. "It makes sense that for women, the area of relationships is where a journey of self-discovery would take place."

"I think everything in a woman's life is relationships," Ruth pointed out. "You know sometimes when I'm in my shop doing a customer's hair and all my other girls are working around me, it feels as if we're all connected." She pointed to the stars on my *Seven Sisters* block. "Like you, I feel as if I'm in the center of all my 'sisters'. I feel as if I'm at the center of this great huge web of relationships. I know people that I don't even know! Do you know what I mean?"

We all nodded.

I understood the feeling she was describing. "Every time someone comes into my shop and buys material to make a quilt for someone else, and they tell me why they are making it, and tell me about the person, I feel as if I have met that person. Sometimes I think I would recognize them if they walked in the door."

Ruth spoke with deep emotion as she struggled with her words. "I've been thinking of leaving Bill," she told us, pausing to take a deep confessional breath. "I have tried and tried to make the relationship work, but it just won't. Every day when I put on my makeup I feel as if I'm putting on a mask to hide my feelings of loneliness and despair. And when I show other women how to do their makeup I wonder if I'm just giving them a mask to wear also. You know, I was tempted to sell out to AJ. I wanted to run away, to leave Clareville." She looked across at me with chagrin. I reached out and patted her arm reassuringly. "But after everything you've said . . ." She took another trembling breath. "I don't think I can. I have to stay here . . . but maybe not with Bill.

Somehow I'll find a way. I have to stay here in the circle of women where I belong. Sure, they may just be customers and employees, but they are the people I'm connected to. Maybe all I do is re-shape their hair and their makeup and make them feel good about themselves, but it's a role for me. It's not because I don't think there's anything else out there for me . . . It's because I'm good at it. It's what I'm supposed to do."

"Your first best destiny," Millie agreed, quoting a famous ex-pression from the *Star Trek* movies.

"That is following your bliss," I pointed out. "People often think that following your bliss is something extraordinary or that it's something ordinary people can't do. But the truth is, it *is* ordinary. It's being the best possible you. It's engaging the world. If you truly follow your bliss, it should be like breathing, without thought and without effort. After all it is just being who you truly are."

Ruth put her hand over her heart. "It's heartening to know that this heroine's journey stuff could be about anyone, that it's about me too."

"That's just the thing," I commented. "Enlightenment is what you experience as you engage everyday life and realize the under-lying truths of existence. It doesn't have to be on the six o'clock news to be heroic. And you don't have to wait for a teacher or guru to come along and give you permission to take the first step."

"That's right," Millie concluded. "If everyone waited until they had all the answers before they began to teach others and make an impact, then no child would ever learn to read. In fact no one would ever have children! You start from wherever you are."

Viola had remained silent through our discussion, but finally she felt compelled to speak. In a near whisper she said, "It was when my dear Calvin died . . ." She sighed deeply.

She could have stopped there. We all felt compassion for her sorrow. Viola and Calvin had been married for forty-eight years.

"My whole life I lived for Cal. We had our ups and downs but we were happy. I could never imagine a day without him. Then he died. And I didn't know what to do. I guess you would say I was thrown rudely into that heroine's journey you're talking about. I had to discover how to live with only one-half of myself. I had to find something to do, some reason to go on living."

My heart went out to her. Forty-eight years, I thought in amazement. Jack and I were only married fourteen years when he died. I couldn't imagine how much more painful it must have been after almost half a century together.

"What did you do?" I asked. "What was your reason for going on?"

"I'm not sure what the reason was," she replied, "But I realized that holding onto a dead love just puts a chain on your heart."

I sucked in my breath as her words went straight to my heart. I remembered my gold chain and locket which lay in my jewelry box.

"The love wasn't dead, but the physical body of the man was. Hold onto the memories, yes, but you can't hold onto life like a frozen layer cake. You have to move on into your own life no matter what it is."

We all fell silent as we contemplated Viola's wisdom.

Ivy had been sitting looking at each of my quilt blocks and then placing them around the cutting table in a circle. "I understand using the traditional patterns because of the symbol or metaphor they represent to you, but why didn't you make one of your own? I mean why didn't you design your own block?"

"I don't know. I guess it never occurred to me. There are hundreds of quilt blocks already in existence. It never dawned on me that I could make one of my own," I answered. It was a good question. It started me thinking and several ideas jumped into my head.

"If a heroine's journey, as you describe it, is a trip out of your old self and into your new self, I would think that you'd have to design a new block to represent the new you at the end of the journey," Marlene observed.

I was taken aback by her words. "You're absolutely right!" I exclaimed. "And all of a sudden I think I have an idea what it should look like. You see, what would I do without all of you? I really hadn't figured out how I would finish the quilt, but now I know. That's the missing block. Thanks."

It was a quiet and contemplative group that broke up slowly that afternoon. Lots of hugs, lots of connectedness. Wasn't that one of the first things that Jo had said? Everything you are seeking, is seeking you.

MY OWN QUILT BLOCK took its place in the center of my memory quilt. It's larger than the others and although it is set in a square, it is a circular block. The circle is an ancient symbol of womanhood and the cycle of life. The circle is a vessel, a receptacle of all things, the circumference of the universe. It is the healing womb of woman and creation where we find wholeness and holiness. As with the flying wheel, as you trace around the circle, there is a descent but it must be followed by an ascent and renewal, as inevitable as the waxing-waning moon. The circle is also a silvery white moon that has expanded into its fullness. A circle of completion. The moon is not a source of light, it merely reflects the light of the sun. Sometimes it is an ample and true reflection, sometimes it is untouched by the light, and between these two states it grows and dies, drawing the spiritually charged ebb and flow of the feminine tides with it.

Inside the circle I pieced a *Tree of Life* motif made of green triangular leaves representing the growth of a heroine's journey. Triangles symbolize the trinity that is the union of mind, body and spirit. Within the tree are the three primary colors of "fruit," the colors that I again used for my three children: red for Jennifer, blue for Robbie, and yellow for Susan. They are full color mature blossoms but they are safely cradled in the arms of the tree of life. I embellished the tree by sewing my gold chain and heart-shaped locket among our children and the growing branches.

Beneath the shade and security of the tree I appliqued the silhouette of an old spirit wolf howling at the moon. Such howling is sometimes done in frustration at the injustice of apparently insurmountable odds. Sometimes a howl is a call to the wildness of our ferocious, unvanquished spirit. Sometimes it's a song that just plain feels good. We don't always have to run from the wolf. We can turn and tame her fierce and loyal spirit. A huntress, yes, but one of survival for the tribe. I am also the wolf. The wolf's voice is my voice. A confident voice howling in communion with the pack.

On the other side, beneath the tree I embroidered a stick woman. I am also the fully round-bodied stick figure beating a little round drum, like Shiva dancing the creative powers into life. To dance is to be alive to the possibilities of creation. To dance is to call forth the power of women with the incessant heartbeat of life. To dance is to follow the thumping hum of the universe. It is the call to attention of a distant drum. There are certain tribes where only the old women have the right to dance. It's considered unseemly for men or young women to dance because to dance is to call forth the powers of creativity. The rhythms of dance are in tune with the rhythm of the universe, so the old women—the women of the thirteenth moon, the menopause moon—are responsible for keeping the tribe in harmony with the universe. Young women are the source of life, the power is within them. They are the power but do not control it. Only old women have the wisdom to control the power and use it for the good of the village.

For the ground beneath the wolf-I and the dancing-I there is an extra piece of "wombat" fur, for the foundation of sisters who give me creative ground to stand on.

It was a very unconventional, free and different sort of block for me. It's unsettling in its innovation and lack of rules. It's also comforting for the same reasons. It tells my story. It is the tapestry of my life. In it I used every stitch technique I know. I have pieced it and appliqued it. I have embellished it and embroidered it.

I have taken every stitch on the path.

I have now only to bind it all together.

ELEVEN

Binding It Together

FOURTH OF JULY. Independence Day. Strains of "It's a Grand Old Flag," "My Country T'is of Thee," and "America the Beautiful." Today was Clareville's day of celebration. Hot dogs. Apple Pie. Candy floss.

And fireworks.

A day-long party was held in the park to celebrate its grand re-opening. There were happy throngs of people everywhere. It seemed as if the whole town turned out. At noon, Mayor Al officially dedicated the new footpaths. As mayor, he along with Millie had been given the honor of buying the first brick and now a new commemorative plaque bearing his name has been added to the south gate nearest the town hall. Big Al was being a lot more opinionated and I was sure his predecessor, Mayor Rimple, would have been pleased. The footpaths were half finished and we were still selling bricks to finish the rest. There would be an appropriately proud photo in the next edition of *The Banner*. All over the park there were carnival rides and games and pony rides for the kids along with free balloons donated by The Emporium. Frank Dempsey reopened his downtown hardware store as an old-fashioned "General Store" selling homemade ice cream, country knickknacks and stationery. Frank himself seemed to enjoy donning a pair of the store's uniform overalls and dishing out sprinkles. From curmudgeon to cracker barrel host, would miracles never cease.

The overalls were Jennifer's idea. She was managing the General Store.

Local artists and craftspeople brought their wares to show and sell. Roving magicians and musicians entertained the crowds. The

Rotarians manned a hot dog and hamburger stand during the afternoon while members of the high school band, wearing their red and black uniforms, played every Sousa march in their repertoire. Viola listened to them all day, her little toes tapping as she had a grand old time. She fell asleep once or twice in one of the folding chairs set out in a great semi-circle around the bandshell that had been hung with red, white and blue bunting. By dinner time the band was red in the face and out of puff. The crowds eventually thinned as everyone headed home for dinner. They would wend their way back in the evening for the concert, fireworks display and dance.

After the fateful Council Meeting, the town plan subcommittee started working and we developed as many ideas as we could. We made a new proposal to Council on the issues which needed official ratification. The angle parking was resolved right away. Within a week town ordinance workers repainted the roads, new street signs were installed, and the local newspaper carried a feature about the changes.

Ivy opened her cafe in the park since that was also a relatively easy project. She obtained her indefinite Temporary Use Permit and was open for business a week later. She negotiated with an outdoor furniture manufacturer to install the white wrought-iron tables and chairs for free, or rather in exchange for advertising on the back of her menu. She continued to be a source of inspirational ideas and hard work. Hiring two cooks for the extra shifts didn't seem to give her any time off. She was as busy as ever.

Since no rezoning was involved, there wasn't much for Council to vote on. In the end, it wasn't about officialdom, it was about the townsfolk. Most of the other matters were in private hands. AJ satisfied his demolition impulses by having the ugly post-war buildings torn down, to everyone's approval. He even donned jeans himself and ran a bulldozer in preparation for paving his new parking lot. That made an interesting front page photo in *The Banner*. He wouldn't make a million dollars overnight but he would make a very comfortable profit from his town real estate. He invested his money in cleaning the Armbruster building, and the Historical Board was assessing the site as a museum. One way or another he was determined to reopen the building to the paying public for the next tourist season. That was okay. Somehow I sensed the continued impassioned voice and determined hand of my daughter behind his actions. Hmmm. Jennifer had begun accepting his dinner invitations again and was no longer leaving in the middle of the meal.

Marlene and Millie formed a happy alliance with the Downtown Merchants' Association and the architects to take on the street front renovation which began as soon as the snow melted. I could tell that the town had returned to normal because "Aunt Ivy" and "Aunt Millie" found a new topic for their epic TV arguments—how "authentic" the renovation should be. Millie supported economics, Ivy supported accuracy. I knew they'd work it out. I just kept goading them into taking action and continuing to move forward by making decisions. As Mother Wombat, I got to do that.

Council voted to form a permanent Town Square Standing Committee to continue to develop and monitor the use of the park facilities. Frank Dempsey came through with paint for the bandshell, as promised. The Rotarians rebuilt and painted it, as promised. Johnson's Nursery replanted the gardens, as promised. So the park became a pretty spiffy place to go. We hadn't come up with a long term solution to the music-in-the-park problem yet, but the theater group is planning to give "Shakespeare in the Park" a try this summer. It took so little for each person or group or business to contribute, but added together everyone produced amazing results. That's leverage for you.

Oh yes, and AJ's other stone house on the corner was renovated. Pierre LaBouche quickly opened his wine bar on the second floor. He kept the dusty stone walls and sawdust on the floor, claiming they added ambiance to his place. I think ambiance is French for cheap atmosphere. He must be right, though. With Pierre's excellent wine cellar and his accent behind "ze bar," it feels quite Continental and sophisticated. It was an immediate success with the trendy young people who go there after work.

Downstairs, Gail and Michael renovated the ground floor and patio for their gourmet restaurant. They kept the low beamed ceiling and the wide plank floors and they cleaned the great stone fireplaces. The restaurant was a success from day one. They called it The Stone House Inn. For a Saturday night, you have to make reservations two weeks in advance. Daniel took me there for dinner to celebrate my first anniversary of Grama's Quilt Shop. The shop is doing really well. I stay open later on Friday and Saturday evenings to catch the rambling downtown summer crowds. I carry more handmade quilts for sale and have some local quilters, including some Amish women, making them to order. I continued Jo's tradition of quilt classes. The Clareville Quilt Guild is working on how we could have an outdoor quilt show in the park next year. Another project under way.

I'm now quilting my Memory Quilt, in between everything else. It sits in a quilt frame in the shop. After I finished the last block I decided to "set" the blocks together with hand-dyed mottled blue sashing. The blue represents the river of life that flows in and around us, that connects us and carries us along on our journeys, from our old selves into our new selves. Without the blue waters there would be no fertile green growth. Saving the trees in the park, saving the blue green planet, had been my metaphor for my stand against the delusion of insignificance. It reminds me that my own world is entwined with the townspeople and the environment. I have learned to engage the world, to accept the challenge.

I'm pleased with the quilt and can't wait to finish it. I have lots of ideas for a new one I want to start. That's the trouble with ideas, they multiply like coat hangers in a closet, and sometimes they're just as tangled together. I guess quilting is addictive but there are worse things a person could become obsessive about. At least quilting is practical. After all, I can keep warm under a quilt. But more importantly, quilting is creative, it opens the mind and heart.

I haven't seen Grama since the council meeting. But I feel her presence in everything I do. Uncle Bernie had lung surgery in

January. We're not sure that he's going to make it. Maybe when Grama's not too busy, she'll drop by again.

This evening's concert began at twilight with the local Sweet Adelines and Barbershop Quartet. Then *Mitch Higley and his Band* played some dixieland jazz until it grew dark and the fireworks began. There was a rollicking display set off by the volunteer firemen in front of the town hall. Everyone oohed and ahed as the explosions lit the sky overhead and boomed in our ears.

It was small town America at its best. It was America's party.

Daniel and I watched the fireworks from the bay window in my apartment and afterward we walked over to the park for the dance. As we stepped into the street I hesitated. Daniel stopped as the tug on his arm alerted him.

"What's wrong?" he asked turning toward me. "Forget something?"

"No," I replied slowly, looking at the park where the trees were lit with festive strings of colored lightbulbs, like it had never been before.

A curious feeling came over me. I had a sudden impulse. "Let's go this way," I suggested and turned left. We walked hand in hand along the sidewalk around the park. When we reached the corner, we saw people going in and out of The Stone House Inn. We turned right and followed the sidewalk until we reached the north gate of the park.

I paused before we passed under the arch. "You know, it's funny," I remarked to Daniel. "All this time. I don't think I've ever entered the park through this gate before—"

"Funny," he agreed, nodding his head.

"Sometimes you get so used to taking the same path every day, you know?"

"Uh huh," he replied and squeezed my hand.

I stepped over and touched the bronze plaque embedded in the stonework. It read, "The future will seek our truth, not just our answers. Dalton J. Rimple, Mayor, 1752."

A chill ran up my spine. It occured to me that Jack must certainly have seen this plaque dozens of times as he grew up in Clareville. I wondered if he had ever stopped to read it. This was Jack's hometown. Unknowingly, he had bequeathed it to me. His legacy was to leave me his love, this town, and this park. By returning to the source of his strength, I was able to launch myself into life again.

I looked at the park where a noisy crowd of people was beginning to gather.

"You okay?" Daniel asked gently.

"Uh huh." I nodded, squeezed his hand and tugged him forward, with me. We passed into the park under the north gate, the gate of the white buffalo and the owl, the gate of wisdom and midnight.

As we approached the bandshell, we saw the country and western band, *Whispering Sage*, setting up. Some high school student volunteers were folding up the chairs and clearing a space in front of the bandshell for dancing. We ran into Ruth and Marlene who were setting up the refreshment table under Ivy's direction. Ruth's husband Bill was busy lugging cases of pop and beer. Months earlier Ruth had drawn the line on Bill and told him to either get help or get out. He decided to get help, and life was taking on a more peaceful nature for Ruth. Marlene had cleared out the bedroom at home which she used as an at-home office and turned it completely into a studio. She's advertising her portrait painting and has had three commissions so far.

When I saw Marlene and Ruth together, I said to Daniel, "You know they remind me of the keys on a piano."

He looked at me curiously. "How so? I know you don't mean because one woman is black and the other is white!"

"No," I said. "It's because they're opposites and yet complementary, and they are tied together. The music of life isn't complete without both of them. One woman finds a way to stay where she is—and make it work. The other finds a way to strike out in a new direction—and make it work. They're bound by the same fragile thread, of coping with who you are and where you are in life."

Daniel nodded thoughtfully. "The fragile thread of dignity and grace that unites the human tapestry—"

I raised my eyes at the curious statement.

Daniel shrugged and grinned sheepishly. "It's a quote from one of my favorite authors, Harper Lee. You know, the woman who wrote *To Kill A Mockingbird*."

I nodded.

"Or maybe I read it in a cartoon—"

More likely, I thought, and grinned.

"I miss Jo," I said wistfully. "She should be here to see the culmination of our efforts."

Daniel squeezed my hand. "I know."

As the first strains of Patsy Cline's *Crazy* drifted across the park, Daniel slipped his arms around me and we began to sway to the music. "I had someone in my shop today asking about my Memory Quilt," I told him as we danced. He hummed in my ear but I knew he was listening. He always did.

"She asked me, 'How do you know when a heroine's journey begins?'"

"And you said?"

"'When you need to put part of your life in a quilt, to tell a story, to understand and make sense of what is happening to you,' I answered her. Then she asked, 'Where does it start?' I told her that it starts from wherever you are. She said, 'But how do you know when one journey ends and another begins?' I said, 'When you reach a feeling of completion, put a border around it and quilt it.'"

"Cra-a-zy for feelin' blue," Daniel sang in my ear. We swayed. We were playing a game. I wanted to talk, he wanted me to dance. I *was* dancing. I can do two things at once.

"So then she asked me, 'What happens when you finish one?' and I told her to just start another. That's life. It isn't one journey but a series of journeys."

"Cra-a-zy for thinkin' aboutchu."

"She said, 'It could be a pretty weird looking quilt,' and I said,

'Yeah, it might be.' And in the end she finally asked me, 'What do you do with it?' I said—"

Daniel loosened his embrace and leaned back slightly, still dancing.

"Leave it for your children's children. It's your legacy. It's the story of who you are," he answered as if it were the most obvious thing in the world.

"That's right," I smiled. "That's it exactly."

The Path of Stitches

An Innocent Sleep
Have Faith

The Wake-up Call to Action
Say "Yes" to the Challenge and the Chaos

The Descent into Trouble
Hold On Until you Hit Bottom

The Threshold of Endless Struggle
Use Your Passion to Give you the Strength to Endure

The Hidden Hands
Tap Every Resource

The Threshold of Worthy Purpose
Have Compassion for All the World

The Final Threshold of Self
Go The Distance

Victory at the Final Threshold
Take Victory as the Starting Point

Assume the Mantle
Tell the Story

Other Books By Starburst Publishers
(Partial Listing—full list available upon request)

The Fragile Thread
Aliske Webb

Aliske Webb, bestselling author of *Twelve Golden Threads*, depicts a touching story that traces a woman's journey of transformation. After burying a husband and raising three children, Aggie reaches mid-life alone and makes a major decision: to move to a small town and open a quilt shop. In the process, she discovers the importance of community and rediscovers her values, beliefs and spiritual foundation. (hardcover)   ISBN 0914984-543   **$17.95**

Why Fret That God Stuff?
Edited by Kathy Collard Miller

Subtitled: *Stories of Encouragement to Help You Let Go and Let God Take Control of All Things in Your Life.* Occasionally, we all become overwhelmed by the everyday challenges of our lives: hectic schedules, our loved ones' needs, unexpected expenses, a sagging devotional life. Why Fret That God Stuff is the perfect beginning to finding joy and peace for the real world!
(trade paper)   ISBN 0914984-500   **$12.95**

God's Unexpected Blessings
Edited by Kathy Collard Miller

Learn to see the *unexpected blessings* in life. These individual essays describe experiences that seem negative on the surface but are something God has used for good in our lives or to benefit others. Witness God at work in our lives. Learn to trust God in action. Realize that we always have a choice to learn and benefit from these experiences by letting God prove His promise of turning all things for our good. (hardcover)   ISBN 0914984-071   **$18.95**

God's Abundance
Edited by Kathy Collard Miller

This day-by-day inspirational is a collection of thoughts by leading Christian writers such as Patsy Clairmont, Jill Briscoe, Liz Curtis Higgs, and Naomi Rhode. *God's Abundance* is based on God's Word for a simpler, yet more abundant life. Learn to make all aspects of your life—personal, business, financial, relationships, even housework a "spiritual abundance of simplicity.
(hardcover)   ISBN 0914984-977   **$19.95**

Promises of God's Abundance
Edited by Kathy Collard Miller

The Bible is filled with God's promises for an abundant life. Promises of God's Abundance for a More Meaningful Life is written in the same way as the bestselling God's Abundance. It will help you discover these promises and show you how simple obedience is the key to an abundant life. Scripture, questions for growth and a simple thought for the day will guide you to a more meaningful life.   ISBN 0914984-098   **$9.95**

A Woman's Guide To Spiritual Power
Nancy L. Dorner
Subtitled: *Through Scriptural Prayer.* Do your prayers seem to go "against a brick wall?" Does God sometimes seem far away or non-existent? If your answer is "Yes," you are not alone. Prayer must be the cornerstone of your relationship to God. "This book is a powerful tool for anyone who is serious about prayer and discipleship."—Florence Littauer
(trade paper)   ISBN 0914984-470   **$9.95**

God's Vitamin "C" for the Spirit of WOMEN
Kathy Collard Miller
Subtitled: *"Tug-at-the-Heart" stories to Inspire and Delight Your Spirit.* A beautiful treasury of timeless stories, quotes, and poetry designed by and for women. Well-known Christian women like Liz Curtis Higgs, Patsy Clairmont, Naomi Rhode, and Elisabeth Elliott share from their hearts on subjects like Marriage, Motherhood, Christian Living, Faith, and Friendship.
(trade paper)   ISBN 0914984-934   **$12.95**

Purchasing Information:
www.starburstpublishers.com

Books are available from your favorite bookstore, either from current stock or special order. To assist bookstore in locating your selection be sure to give title, author, and ISBN #. If unable to purchase from the bookstore you may order direct from STARBURST PUBLISHERS. When ordering enclose full payment plus $3.00 for shipping and handling ($4.00 if Canada or overseas). Payment in U.S. Funds only. Please allow two to three weeks minimum (longer overseas) for delivery. Make checks payable to and mail to: STARBURST PUBLISHERS, P.O. Box 4123, LANCASTER, PA 17604. Credit card orders may also be placed by calling 1-800-441-1456 (credit card orders only), Mon-Fri, 8:30 A.M.—5:30 P.M. Eastern Standard Time. Prices subject to change without notice. Catalog available for a 9 x 12 self-addressed envelope with 4 first-class stamps.